SENSATIONAL 60's QUIZ BOOK

BRIAN WILLIAMS

Miles Kelly
PUBLISHING

First published in 2000 by
Miles Kelly Publishing Ltd
Bardfield Centre
Great Bardfield
Essex CM7 4SL

24681097531

ISBN 1 90294 723 1

Editor Keith Parish
Editorial Assistant Mark Darling
Cover Design GardnerQuainton
Design Management Jo Brewer
Page Layout Helen Weller
Production Rachel Jones

INTRODUCTION

Those who remember the 60s – and for many they are just a smoky blur – will summon up images, as they tackle these quizzes, of flared hipsters, Cuban heels, cheese-cloth shirts, Zapata moustaches and war department overcoats. Strains of *Flowers in the Rain*, *A Whiter Shade of Pale*, *Telstar* and *Big Girls Don't Cry*, will come limping into their inner ears. They may even recall names like Milton Obote, Jack Ruby and Archbishop Makarios and the achievements of Rod Laver, Denis Law and Anne Packer. If they were there they will remember for certain the Moon landing and (just possibly) the names of the astronauts, but what about the year of the Torrey Canyon disaster or the year that Swedish drivers started to drive on the right? Much trickier.

If you never lived through the 60s or have zero recollection of them, these quizzes will be a helter skelter ride of people, events and 'happenings'. The names, in many cases, will have a strangely familiar ring to them.

Whether you were there in body and soul or not, you are about to become an expert on the century's most exciting and sensational decade.

QUIZ 1
POT LUCK

· ·

1 Which sportsman's nickname was "Broadway Joe"?

2 Who played Blofeld in *You Only Live Twice*?

3 What colour was his cat?

4 In which country was poet Peter Porter born?

5 Which future political heavyweight was working for the National Union of Seamen in 1968?

6 For which TV show did Allan Plater write many scripts?

7 Which Eastbourne doctor suspected of killing his patients was reinstated by the Medical Council in 1961?

8 Who joined BBC Radio in 1969, with a degree in Scandinavian studies?

9 Which field marshal and adviser to Churchill died in 1963?

10 Whom did Angus Ogilvy marry in 1963?

11 Who was the bride's mother?

12 For what was Bill Brandt famous?

13 For what was Mancunian Joe Brown renowned?

14 Which poet wrote *Briggflats* (1966)?

15 Which tall comic actor, born in Weston super Mare, appeared in *The Frost Report*?

· ·

ANSWERS

1, Joe Namath 2, Donald Pleasence 3, White 4, Australia 5, John Prescott 6, *Z Cars* 7, John Bodkin Adams 8, Kate Adie 9, Viscount Alanbrooke 10, Princess Alexandra 11, Princess Marina of Kent 12, Photographing nudes 13, Mountain climbing 14, Basil Bunting 15, John Cleese

PEOPLE

. . . .

1 King Freddie (died 1969) was the ruler or Kabaka of… where?

2 Which British Labour Party leader died in 1963?

3 Who succeeded him as party leader?

4 Of which country was Zog (died 1960) the former king?

5 What award did Albert Luthuli of South Africa win in 1960?

6 Which Swedish diplomat was awarded a posthumous Nobel Prize?

7 In which part of Africa had he been trying to bring peace?

8 Which American was awarded the 1964 Nobel peace prize?

9 Lord Alexander of Tunis died in June 1969. Was he a famous soldier, explorer or archaeologist?

10 Which Hollywood sex symbol died in August 1962?

11 Who was the first artistic boss of the Royal Shakespeare Company?

12 Which wartime leader died in 1965?

13 Where was he buried?

14 This was near his birthplace, which was?

15 Who became Britain's youngest-ever Member of Parliament when elected in 1969?

. . . .

ANSWERS

1. Buganda (in Africa) 2, Hugh Gaitskell 3, Harold Wilson 4, Albania 5, Nobel Prize for peace 6, Dag Hammarskjold 7, The Congo 8, Martin Luther King 9, Soldier (a World War II commander) 10, Marilyn Monroe 11, Peter Hall 12, Sir Winston Churchill 13, Bladon in Oxfordshire 14, Blenheim Palace 15, Bernadette Devlin

QUIZ 3
ARTS & ENTERTAINMENT

· ·

1 Which American writer was awarded the 1962 Nobel Prize for literature?

2 A French philosopher refused the 1964 Nobel Prize for literature. Who was he?

3 What was the title of a 1967 bestseller about human behaviour?

4 Who was the author?

5 Which novel was the subject of an obscenity trial in 1960?

6 Who was its author?

7 Did he take part in the trial?

8 The author of *A Town Like Alice* and *On the Beach* died in January 1960. Who was he?

9 Which satirical magazine first appeared in Britain in 1962?

10 French novelist Albert Camus died in 1960. How?

11 In which country was playwright Samuel Beckett born?

12 Which honour did he receive in 1969?

13 The creator of James Bond died of a heart attack in 1964. Who was he?

14 Who wrote *Catch-22*?

15 On which Shakespeare play was the musical *West Side Story* based?

· ·

ANSWERS

1, John Steinbeck 2, Jean-Paul Sartre 3, *The Naked Ape* 4, Desmond Morris 5, *Lady Chatterley's Lover* 6, D H Lawrence 7, No, he died in 1930 8, Nevil Shute 9, *Private Eye* 10, He was killed in a car crash 11, Ireland 12, Nobel Prize for literature 13, Ian Fleming 14, Joseph Heller 15, *Romeo and Juliet*

WORLD EVENTS
1960

. . . .

1 On which river was a new flood barrier plan announced in 1960?

2 Where was Lar, hit by an earthquake?

3 Where did President Rhee's cabinet resign?

4 From which country did Togoland become independent?

5 On which continent was Togoland?

6 Of which country was Adenauer head of state?

7 Of which dam did Nasser lay the foundation stone?

8 Where was Little Rock?

9 Who launched the world's longest liner?

10 What was it named?

11 Which British colony gained its independence in June?

12 Who was first prime minister of the Congo?

13 Where was the 1960 US Democratic Convention held?

14 Who was chosen to be presidential candidate?

15 What method of dating ancient objects was pioneered by 1960 Nobel prizewinner Willard F. Libby?

. . . .

ANSWERS

15, Radiocarbon dating
11, Somaliland 12, Patrice Lumumba 13, Los Angeles 14, John F Kennedy
7, Aswan High Dam 8, Arkansas, USA 9, Madame De Gaulle 10, France
1,The Thames 2, Iran 3, South Korea 4, France 5, Africa 6, West Germany

QUIZ 5
POT LUCK
1960

● ●

1 What did the Pope tell Catholics not to watch if the Vatican judged them "unsafe"?

2 Which bridegroom-to-be was the son of the Countess of Rosse?

3 What did aviation minister Duncan Sandys say Britain would build?

4 Where were private businesses nationalized?

5 Which royal prince was born on 19 February?

6 What were his full names?

7 In which continent was Nyasaland?

8 What invention of 1960 was credited to Theodore Maiman?

9 In which English county was the Jodrell Bank radio telescope built?

10 Who starred in this year's Oscar-winning movie *Ben-Hur*?

11 How many Oscars did the film win?

12 Which South African leader was wounded by a gunman?

13 Where was the 1960 European Cup final played before 135,000 soccer fans?

14 Which two famous car makers merged?

15 How much was a pint of beer in August 1960 (in old or decimal money)?

● ●

ANSWERS

1. Television programmes 2. Antony Armstrong-Jones 3. A supersonic airliner 4. Cuba 5. Prince Andrew 6. Andrew Albert Christian Edward 7. Africa 8. The laser 9. Cheshire 10. Charlton Heston 11. Ten 12. South Africa's prime minister Hendrik Verwoerd 13. Hampden Park, Glasgow 14. Jaguar and Daimler 15. 1s 7d (one shilling and seven pence, roughly 8p in today's money)

QUIZ 6
PEOPLE

. . . .

1 What was Beatle Ringo's real name?

2 Who was the oldest Beatle?

3 And the youngest?

4 Who became Britain's first West Indian life peer in 1969?

5 In which sport had he been a star?

6 Levi Eshkol died in 1969; of which country was he prime minister?

7 How did Scotland and Spurs soccer star John White die in 1963?

8 Which former US President died in March 1969?

9 Which World War II campaign had he commanded?

10 What his nickname?

11 Was he a Republican or a Democrat?

12 Which British businessman was exchanged for Soviet spy Gordon Lonsdale in 1964?

13 At which Olympic Games did America's Wilma Rudolph star?

14 How many gold medals did she win?

15 At which Welsh university did the Prince of Wales attend a course in 1969?

. . . .

ANSWERS

1. Richard Starkey 2. John Lennon (9/10/40) 3. George Harrison (25/2/43) 4. Sir Learie Constantine 5. Cricket 6. Israel 7. He was hit by lightning on a golf course 8. Dwight Eisenhower 9. The Allied invasion of France in 1944 10. Ike 11. Republican 12. Greville Wynne 13. Rome 1960 14. Three 15. Aberystwyth

QUIZ 7
ARTS & ENTERTAINMENT

1 J… T…, American satirical writer, died in November 1961. His name?

2 His most famous work was about a daydreamer; what was its title?

3 What was the title of the Liverpool music paper first produced in 1961?

4 How did writer Ernest Hemingway meet his death in 1961?

5 Which non-Australians played Australians in the 1960 movie *The Sundowners*?

6 Which movie "king" died in 1960?

7 Which British TV channel began broadcasting in 1964?

8 On which American TV show did the Beatles make a famous appearance in 1964?

9 The "silent" Marx brother died in 1964. Who was he?

10 Who directed the 1969 film *Oh What a Lovely War*?

11 Which of the following actors was not in *Oh What a Lovely War*: Laurence Olivier, Dirk Bogarde, Ralph Richardson, Richard Burton?

12 Which two movie superstars married in 1964?

13 Who wrote *The Valley of the Dolls*?

14 Who wrote *Portnoy's Complaint*?

15 Who took over Marilyn Monroe's part in the 1962 film *Something's Got to Give*, after Monroe's death?

ANSWERS

1, James Thurber 2, *The Secret Life of Walter Mitty* 3, Mersey Beat 4, He committed suicide (or shot himself accidentally while cleaning a gun) 5, Robert Mitchum and Deborah Kerr 6, Clark Gable 7, BBC 2 8, *The Ed Sullivan Show* 9, Harpo 10, Richard Attenborough 11, Richard Burton 12, Elizabeth Taylor and Richard Burton 13, Jacqueline Susann 14, Philip Roth 15, Doris Day

QUIZ 8
WORLD EVENTS
1969

• •

1 To which part of the United Kingdom were troops deployed in 1969 to keep the peace?

2 Who was Britain's Home Secretary?

3 Which US senator became Democrat whip in January?

4 Whose trial for murder was held in Los Angeles?

5 Who was sworn in as the 37th President of the United States?

6 Which ice hockey result sparked off anti-Communist demonstrations?

7 With which ship did the US destroyer "Frank E Evans" collide in June?

8 Which European country was led by Jack Lynch?

9 Who were honoured with tickertape parades through New York and Chicago in August?

10 What did Harvard Medical School report it had isolated one of?

11 Of which country did Lon Nol become premier in August?

12 Which country was the world's leading coal-producer?

13 Of which country had Joseph Kasavubu, who died in March, been president?

14 Who was his political rival, reported dead in 1969, two years after being kidnapped?

15 In which Commonwealth country did English and French become joint official languages?

• •

ANSWERS

QUIZ 9
PEOPLE

. . . .

1 Who first walked London's streets in 1960?

2 For what had Irene Castle, died 1969, been famous?

3 What was her husband and stage partner's name?

4 Of which country did Julius Nyerere become prime minister?

5 Which member of the royal family shot an Indian tiger in 1961?

6 Which two Western leaders enjoyed a "special relationship"?

7 Who said "Ask not what your country can do for you, but what you can do for your country"?

8 Who was named Archbishop of Canterbury in 1961?

9 Which Indian leader died in 1964?

10 Which part of the globe did Wally Herbert walk across in 1969?

11 For what crimes was Adolf Eichmann tried in 1960?

12 Who was the unfortunate passenger in a car on Chapaquiddick Island on 18 July 1969?

13 Which politician was with her?

14 Which lord became British prime minister on 18 October 1963?

15 Which artist was honoured in 1969 with an exhibition to mark the 300th anniversary of his death?

. . . .

ANSWERS

QUIZ 10
ARTS & ENTERTAINMENT

. . . .

1 Who pursued Mai Zetterling in the 1961, comedy *Only Two Can Play*?

2 What was the title of Mario Puzo's novel about the Mafia?

3 Who starred as a stripper in *Gypsy*?

4 Who was The Birdman of Alcatraz on screen?

5 Who wrote *The Making of the President*?

6 Complete the title of this 1969 novel: *The Beastly Beatitudes of* ...?

7 And the author?

8 Which actress made her name in *A Taste of Honey*?

9 Complete the 1962 film title: *Last Year in* ...?

10 Who starred in the film of the musical *The Music Man*: a) Robert Preston b) Paul Newman or c) Fred Astaire?

11 *Lolita* was a 1962 screen hit; who wrote the novel?

12 Who played Lolita in this film?

13 Who played the captain in the 1962 film of *Mutiny on the Bounty*?

14 What was the captain's name?

15 Was Frank O'Connor best known for writing stories, playing golf, or telling jokes on television?

. . . .

ANSWERS

1. Peter Sellers 2. *The Godfather* 3. Natalie Wood 4. Burt Lancaster 5. Theodore H White 6. *Balthazar* B 7. J P Donleavy 8. Rita Tushingham 9. *Marienbad* 10. a) Robert Preston 11. Vladimir Nabokov 12. Sue Lyon 13. Trevor Howard 14. Captain Bligh 15. Writing stories

QUIZ 11
WORLD EVENTS

. . . .

1 What was President Kennedy's middle name?

2 In which city was a Reuters correspondent kept under house arrest for 26 months?

3 What was his name?

4 What did the initials SALT stand for?

5 Which countries signed such an agreement in 1969?

6 Where?

7 Which Asian war leader died in 1969?

8 From which country was King Idris deposed in 1969?

9 Who was named as heir to Mao Tse-tung in 1969?

10 What was Sri Lanka called in the 60s?

11 Of which Caribbean island did Ronald Webster become leader in 1969?

12 Whose country's prime minister was Olof Palme?

13 Which South American country had a President called Ovando Candia?

14 Golda Meir became prime minister of Israel, but where was she born?

15 Which illness came in epidemic form from Hong Kong in 1968?

. . . .

ANSWERS

1. Fitzgerald 2. Beijing (China) 3. Anthony Grey 4. SALT stood for Strategic Arms Limitation Treaty 5. USA and USSR 6. Helsinki 7. Ho Chi Minh of North Vietnam 8. Libya 9. Lin Piao 10. Ceylon 11. Anguilla 12. Sweden's 13. Bolivia 14. Kiev in the Ukraine 15. Influenza

QUIZ 12
SPORT

. . . .

1 Damon's dad was world motor racing champion in 1962. Name?

2 Next year another British driver won the title. Who?

3 Which British player triumphed in the 1969 Wimbledon women's singles final?

4 Which club did Leicester City sell soccer player Allan Clarke in 1969 for a British record fee of £166,700?

5 Tamara Press was a controversial Soviet female athletics star. Why?

6 With which team of Blues was Tommy Docherty a 60s soccer coach?

7 Was the Lotus Climax of 1960 a Grand Prix car, a pop band, or a book about sexual technique?

8 In which sport was Neil Fox a 60s star?

9 Which team of footballing Sky Blues rose from the depths to the English First Division?

10 In which sport was Willie Shoemaker a 60s celebrity?

11 Which fiery fast bowler took 132 wickets to help Yorkshire win the 1960 cricket county championship?

12 Which race was won by Merryman II in 1960?

13 What did Henry Cooper give up in 1969 a) smoking b) soccer c) the British heavyweight boxing title?

14 Which Australian athlete was the star distance runner of 1968 but finished only 5th in the Olympic 5000-metres final?

15 Where were the 1960 Winter Olympics held?

. . . .

ANSWERS

1, Graham Hill 2, Jim Clark 3, Ann Jones 4, Leeds United 5, Doubters questioned whether she was a woman 6, Chelsea 7, A Grand Prix car 8, Rugby League 9, Coventry City 10, Horse racing (America's leading jockey) 11, Fred Trueman 12, The Grand National 13, c) the British heavyweight boxing title 14, Ron Clarke 15, Squaw Valley, Idaho

QUIZ 13
PEOPLE

. . . .

1 Which spy escaped from prison in London in 1966?

2 Which prison did he flee from?

3 And where did he turn up?

4 How did spaceman Yuri Gagarin die?

5 In which year?

6 Which Right-wing US politician lost the 1964 presidential election?

7 Who was the victor?

8 Which Engish cricketing knight died on 21 December 1963?

9 For which county did he play?

10 In which city was Martin Luther King murdered in April 1968?

11 Who was charged with the killing?

12 What year was Robert Kennedy assassinated?

13 Who was found guilty of shooting Robert Kennedy?

14 Where was the Robert Kennedy shooting: a) Chicago b) Houston c) Los Angeles?

15 Which British politician attracted notoriety for his "rivers of blood" speech in 1968?

. . . .

ANSWERS

1.George Blake 2.Wormwood Scrubs 3.The Soviet Union 4.In a plane crash
5.1968 6.Barry Goldwater 7.Lyndon Johnson 8.Sir Jack Hobbs 9.Surrey
10.Memphis,Tennessee 11.James Earl Ray 12.1968 13.Sirhan Sirhan
14.(c) Los Angeles 15.Enoch Powell

QUIZ 14
POT LUCK

- -

1 Which Irish politician said (allegedly) "What we need is another Cromwell"?

2 Whose wife was Queen Fabiola?

3 Who said: "Politicians promise to build a bridge when there is no river"?

4 Which Archbishop of Canterbury met the Pope in December 1960?

5 Which British actress played Katherine in *The Taming of the Shrew* at Stratford?

6 Which country launched its first space rocket in January 1961?

7 Which famous animal died in Kenya in 1961?

8 Which British car reached the "1 million made" mark in 1965?

9 What speed became the legal maximum on British roads in 1965?

10 What slogan was used to promote British goods and businesses during 1969–70?

11 When was Prince Charles invested as Prince of Wales?

12 Where did the ceremony take place?

13 Which Christmas favourite was missing from British TV screens in 1969?

14 Two Russian cosmonauts had to fight off hungry wolves after landing from a 1965 spaceflight. True or false?

15 Which was Britain's first seven-sided coin, first minted in 1969?

- -

ANSWERS

1. Ian Paisley 2. King Baudouin of the Belgians 3. Khrushchev 4. Dr Geoffrey Fisher 5. Peggy Ashcroft 6. Italy 7. Elsa the lioness 8. The Mini 9. 70 mph 10. I'm backing Britain 11. 1969 12. Caernarvon Castle 13. The Queen's message 14. True (Alexei Leonov and Pavel Belyaev came down off-course in a forest) 15. The 50p piece

QUIZ 15
WORLD EVENTS
AFRICA

1 Which African civil war began in July 1967?
2 Which African state was ruled by Kwame Nkrumah until February 1966?
3 In which country was politician Tom Mboya assassinated in 1969?
4 Eduardo Mondlane was the leader of the FRELIMO guerrillas – in which country?
5 Of which African country was Seretse Khama leader?
6 In which country did General Mobutu seize power in 1965?
7 In which African country did Nimeiry lead a coup in 1968?
8 Who won Zambia's first post-independence election, in 1968?
9 In which country was there tension between Kikuyu and Luo groups?
10 Where did President Sekou Touré hold power?
11 On which island was the Malagasy Republic founded?
12 In which country was the Bureau of State Security known as BOSS?
13 In which colony was there an oil-rich region called Cabinda?
14 And which European power still ruled there?
15 On which river was the Cahorabassa hydroelectric scheme planned?

ANSWERS

1, The Biafran war in Nigeria 2, Ghana 3, Kenya 4, Mozambique 5, Botswana 6, The Congo 7, The Sudan 8, Kenneth Kaunda 9, Kenya 10, Guinea 11, Madagascar 12, South Africa 13, Angola 14, Portugal 15, The Zambezi

QUIZ 16
PEOPLE

. . . .

1 Name the three astronauts who circled the Moon in 1968.
a) Frank ... b) Jim ... c) Bill ...

2 Who was the first Roman Catholic President of the United States?

3 This president was also the youngest: true or false?

4 Which South African leader was jailed in 1962?

5 Which Soviet leader confronted the West in the Cuban missile crisis?

6 Patsy Kline was killed in a plane crash in 1963; as what was she famous?

7 What was the name of John and Cynthia Lennon's baby, born 8 April 1963?

8 Was Yves Saint-Martin a famous 60s jockey, fashion designer, or lone sailor?

9 Was Billy Strayhorn, who died in 1967, famous as a musician, politician or actor?

10 With whose band did Billy Strayhorn work as a composer?

11 Who made his debut for Manchester United in 1963?

12 How did boxer Rocky Marciano die in 1969?

13 Was Milton Friedman a) an economist b) a comedian or c) a track athlete?

14 Which hurdler was BBC Sportsman of the Year in 1966?

15 Where was Thor Heyerdahl born?

. . . .

ANSWERS

1, a) Frank Borman, b) James Lovell, c) Bill Anders 2, John F Kennedy 3, True 4, Nelson Mandela 5, Khruschev 6, Country and western singer 7, Julian 8, Jockey 9, Musician 10, Duke Ellington 11, George Best 12, Plane crash 13, a) an economist 14, David Hemery 15, Norway

POT LUCK

. . . .

1 What was Donald Crowhurst doing when he disappeared in 1969?

2 Which two countries fought a "Soccer War"?

3 In what year?

4 Which star of the 1963 epic *Cleopatra* wore 65 costumes?

5 Which London landmark was cleaned in 1968, for the first time since 1844?

6 By what name was detective writer "Nicholas Blake" better known?

7 Whcih defence organization was disbanded in 1968?

8 Who played the photographer in *Blow Up*?

9 What were there 3.4 billion of in 1967?

10 Which stretch of water did John Fairfax row in 1969?

11 Which British daily newspaper closed in 1960, merging with the Daily Mail?

12 Which historic route was cracked by the oil tanker "Manhattan" in 1969?

13 What did the initials CND stand for?

14 What year did colour TV begin on BBC-1 and ITV in the United Kingdom?

15 Which breed was Britain's most popular dairy cow in the late 1960s?

. . . .

ANSWERS

1, Taking part in a round the world yacht race 2, El Salvador and Honduras 3, 1969 4, Elizabeth Taylor 5, Nelson's Column 6, Cecil Day-Lewis 7, The Civil Defence Corps in Britain 8, David Hemmings 9, People in the world 10, The Atlantic Ocean 11, The News Chronicle 12, The North West Passage 13, Campaign for Nuclear Disarmament 14, 1969 15, Friesian (more than 60%)

WORLD EVENTS

. . . .

1 What post did Warren Burger hold?

2 Where were 9 million people on strike in 1968?

3 Who took "one small step" in July 1969?

4 Who succeeded Nasser as president of Egypt?

5 Which church gathering met for the 10th time in 1968?

6 Whom did Pierre Trudeau succeed in 1968?

7 As what of where?

8 Which Australian prime minister died in 1967?

9 How did he die?

10 Which French university saw riots in 1968?

11 In which city were plans for a Post Office Tower announced in 1961?

12 Who in 1961 was elected Oxford's professor of poetry?

13 Which telescope bounced signals off the Moon?

14 Where was Stanleyville?

15 What did De Gaulle plan to give Algerians?

. . . .

ANSWERS

1. Chief Justice of the United States, 2. France 3. Neil Armstrong (on the Moon) 4. Sadat 5. The Lambeth Conference 6. Lester Pearson 7. Prime minister of Canada 8. Harold Holt 9. He drowned 10. The Sorbonne (Paris) 11. London 12. Robert Graves 13. Jodrell Bank 14. The Congo 15. Home rule

QUIZ 19
SPORT

. . . .

1 What did Andy Granatelli design: a) racing cars b) yachts c) soccer boots?

2 Which team were US professional basketball champions every year from 1960 to 1966?

3 Which basketball team ended this winning run in the 1966–67 season?

4 Which Australian tennis player won the 1960 US men's singles title?

5 Which event did David Hemery win a gold medal in the 1968 Olympics?

6 Which sport's 60s championships were sponsored by the Federation Internationale des Quilleurs (FIQ)?

7 The top goalscorer in English League soccer in 1963–64 played for Carlisle United! Name?

8 What nationality was racing driver Jochen Rindt?

9 Which Australian tennis player won Wimbledon in 1961 and 1962 before turning professional?

10 When did he next win the Wimbledon title?

11 Which soccer star moved from Torino to Manchester United in 1962 for £115,000?

12 Armin Hary ran 100 metres in a world record 10 seconds in 1960; what nationality was he?

13 Wes Hall and Charlie Griffiths were a speedy duo; were they a) cricket bowlers b) rowers or c) Monte Carlo Rally drivers?

14 Which country provided the 1960 Olympic Marathon winner?

15 Who was he?

. . . .

ANSWERS

1, a) Racing cars, for the Indy 500 races 2, Boston Celtics 3, Philadelphia 76ers 4, Neale Fraser 5, 400-metres hurdles 6, Ten-pin bowling 7, Hugh McIlmoyle 8, Austrian 9, Rod Laver 10, 1968 11, Denis Law 12, East German 13 a) West Indies fast bowlers 14, Ethiopia 15, Abebe Bikila

QUIZ 20
PEOPLE

. . . .

1 Which country was led by Norman Manley?

2 Which school did Prince Charles leave in 1962?

3 Which school did he attend between 1962 and 1967?

4 In which European city was "Apollo 11" astronaut Michael Collins born?

5 The Reverend William Keble Martin's claim to fame was a) a book about the Church of England b) British plant life or c) a history of cricket?

6 What was Osbert Lancaster famous as?

7 Was John Dover Wilson a) a Shakespeare scholar or b) a former captain of the England rugby team?

8 This World War II general died in 1969, as Earl Alexander of…?

9 What organization did Allen Dulles head until 1961?

10 Who was Philip Blaiberg, who died August 1969?

11 How long had he survived?

12 Whose husband was Leonard Woolf, who died in 1969?

13 Who sang in comeback concerts at the London Palladium and Carnegie Hall in 1960?

14 Who came second in the 1963 ballot for the Labour Party leadership?

15 Who came first?

. . . .

ANSWERS

15, Harold Wilson
12, Virginia Woolf, the writer 13, Judy Garland 14, George Brown
Agency 10, A heart transplant patient 11, 19 months with a new heart
6, Cartoonist 7, a) a Shakespeare scholar 8, Tunis 9, The Central Intelligence
1, Jamaica 2, Cheam 3, Gordonstoun 4, Rome 5, b) *The Concise British Flora*

QUIZ 21
POT LUCK

- -

1 What ran for the last time on 11 August 1968 in Britain?

2 Whose widow was Princess Marina, who died in 1968?

3 What was the name of Britain's first nuclear submarine?

4 For which crime was Ronald Biggs convicted in 1964?

5 Which river became associated with a pop music sound in the early 60s?

6 What year was the Cuban missile crisis?

7 Which new British cathedral was consecrated in 1962?

8 What year did "Apollo 12" land on the Moon?

9 What was Colin Cowdrey's first name?

10 Which southern African country became independent in 1968?

11 What kind of baby animal was London Zoo's Pipaluk?

12 Which building was a new addition to London's Heathrow airport in 1969?

13 In 1969 the US government signed contracts to build the F-14 and F-15. What were they?

14 Which London street became world-famous in the 60s as a fashion icon and tourist hotspot?

15 What was Moon astronaut "Buzz" Aldrin's two first names?

- -

ANSWERS

1. Steam trains 2. The Duke of Kent's 3. "Dreadnought" 4. His part in the Great Train Robbery of 1963 5. The Mersey ("Merseybeat") 6. 1962 7. Coventry 8. 1969 (November) 9. Michael 10. Swaziland 11. A polar bear 12. Terminal One 13. Fighter planes 14. Carnaby Street 15. Edwin Eugene

QUIZ 22
PEOPLE

· ·

1 Who was Vito Genovese: a) a racing driver b) a singer
c) a Mafia boss?

2 Which country got Nicolae Ceaucescu as its president in 1969?

3 Which prince sat in a dustbin in 1969?

4 What office did James Chichester-Clark take on in May 1969?

5 What was Denton Cooley's claim to fame in the medical world?

6 Which British minister decided "no more new universities" in 1965?

7 Which 60s tycoon was born Jan Ludvik Hoch?

8 He became a Labour MP in 1964: true or false?

9 In what artistic field was Rudolf Bing a law unto himself?

10 Was Boris Spassky a champion in a) chess b) bridge or
c) weightlifting?

11 In which country was Franz Josef Strauss a leading politician?

12 Catholic reformer Cardinal Suenens was a) Irish b) Belgian or
c) American?

13 Who became premier of France in 1962?

14 Nelson Rockefeller was governor of which US state?

15 Who rose to prominence as leader of the Free Presbyterian Church
of Ulster?

· ·

ANSWERS

13, Georges Pompidou 14, New York 15, Ian Paisley
Maxwell 8, True 9, Opera 10, a) Chess 11, West Germany 12, b) Belgian
Northern Ireland 5, He was a heart surgeon 6, Anthony Crosland 7, Robert
1 c) a Mafia boss 2, Romania 3, Prince Charles (on stage) 4, Prime minister of

QUIZ 23
ARTS & ENTERTAINMENT

1. *The Longest Day* was a film about which wartime episode?

2. Which film of an 18th-century Henry Fielding novel starred Albert Finney and Susannah York?

3. In which 60s film did POW Steve McQueen attempt to ride a motorbike to freedom?

4. Which press baron's memoirs were titled *Strictly Personal*?

5. In the film *Cleopatra*, who played Julius Caesar?

6. Who was the star of the 1963 movie *Hud*?

7. Complete this 1963 film title: *63 Days at …*?

8. At number and fraction made a famous Fellini film title of 1963; what was it?

9. What was the (short version) title of Stanley Kubrick's 1963 film about nuclear war?

10. The star of the Western *Shane* died in 1964; who was he?

11. Which poet published *Notes to the Hurrying Man* (1969)?

12. *The People's War* was a book about which war?

13. And its author?

14. Which TV comedy series starring Cleese, Palin, Jones and others got its first airing in 1969?

15. Which novelist wrote a "Children of Violence" cycle of novels?

ANSWERS

1. The D-Day landings 2, *Tom Jones* 3, *The Great Escape* 4, Cecil King 5, Rex Harrison 6, Paul Newman 7, *Peking* 8, 8½ 9, *Dr Strangelove* 10, Alan Ladd 11, Brian Patten 12, World War II 13, Angus Calder 14, *Monty Python's Flying Circus* 15, Doris Lessing

QUIZ 24
POT LUCK

. . . .

1 Japan's Kobe Zoo bred a leopon in 1969. What was this animal?

2 What was the "Amsterdam", uncovered in 1969?

3 Where was it found?

4 Why did dogs pull Mounties for the last time in 1969?

5 What was Cilla Black's job at the Cavern Club when she was spotted by John Lennon?

6 At which Welsh singer was it not unusual for female fans to hurl their knickers on-stage?

7 Which organization celebrated its 50th birthday on 1 April 1968?

8 What kind of sport went on at Germany's Nurburgring?

9 In what part of the world was the Crater district a dangerous place to be in 1967?

10 Why did the "Torrey Canyon" hit the headlines in 1967?

11 Which party won the 1964 general election in the UK?

12 Whose sword was used to knight lone sailor Sir Francis Chichester in 1967?

13 Who were the 60s rivals (sometimes fighting rivals) of Rockers?

14 Which 60s prime minister was married to Gladys Mary Baldwin?

15 For which crimes were Ian Brady and Myra Hindley convicted in 1966?

. . . .

ANSWERS

1. A cross between a male leopard and a female lion 2. An 18th-century Dutch ship 3. Offshore from Hastings, England 4. The Royal Canadian Mounted Police made its last spring patrol with dog sleds 5. She was a hat-check girl 6. Tom Jones 7. The Royal Air Force 8. Motor racing 9. Aden (at the time of terrorist campaign) 10. It was an oil tanker that created a major oil spill 11. Labour 12. Sir Francis Drake's 13. Mods 14. Harold Wilson 15. The Moors Murders

QUIZ 25
SPORT

. . . .

1 What year did Wolverhampton Wanderers win the FA Cup: 1960, 1962 or 1964?

2 In which event did Bjorn Wirkola set a world record in 1966?

3 In which sport was Australia's Stuart Mackenzie a world champion?

4 Which horse won the 1960 Derby?

5 Terry Bly was English football's top scorer in 1961. How many goals did he score?

6 And which club did he play for?

7 In which running event did Derek Clayton of Australia set records?

8 The 1960 European Cup final was a thriller; who were the two soccer teams?

9 What was the score?

10 One of the stars of the 1960 European Cup-winning team was Di Stefano; was he Spanish, Argentinian or Italian?

11 In 1961, which soccer team became the first in the 20th century to do the English League and Cup double?

12 Who captained this memorable side?

13 Nicole Duclos was a track star of the 60s; what was her main event?

14 And what country did she represent?

15 Two British women met in the 1961 Wimbledon singles final; who were they?

. . . .

ANSWERS

1. 1960 2. Ski jumping 3. Rowing (sculling) 4. St Paddy 5. 52 6. Peterborough United 7. Marathon 8. Eintracht Frankfurt and Real Madrid 9. 7-3 to Real Madrid 10. Argentinian 11. Tottenham Hotspur 12. Danny Blanchflower 13. 400 metres 14. France 15. Angela Mortimer and Christine Truman

QUIZ 26
WORLD EVENTS

· ·

1 Whom did Dimitric Tsfondas assassinate in 1966?

2 Where did the killing take place?

3 Who or what was Ham?

4 Who found old bones in Olduvai Gorge?

5 Which country left the Commonwealth in 1961?

6 Who was Sir Roy Welensky?

7 Which tragedy occurred in the Ambassador Hotel, Los Angeles in 1968?

8 Which war broke out on 5 June 1967?

9 In which region of the world?

10 And who won the war?

11 Who flew into space aboard "Vostok 6" in 1963?

12 Who was the first president of Uganda?

13 What year did he take office?

14 Who voted in 1967 to stay British?

15 What changes to the British mail came in 1968?

· ·

ANSWERS

1, South African prime minister Hendrik Verwoerd 2, In Parliament in Cape Town 3, A chimpanzee flown into space by the Americans 4, The Leakeys (Louis and Mary) 5, South Africa 6, Prime Minister of the Central African Federation 7, The shooting of Robert Kennedy 8, The Six Day War 9, The Middle East 10, Israel 11, Valentina Tereshkova 12, Milton Obote 13, 1967 14, The people of Gibraltar 15, First and second class stamps

PEOPLE

. . . .

1 Whose presidential campaign was managed by John Mitchell?

2 What year did Edward Kennedy become a US Senator?

3 Whose term did he complete?

4 What was the name of the U-2 spy plane pilot swopped in 1962?

5 For whom was he exchanged?

6 And who released him?

7 Which British spy ring was broken in 1961?

8 Can you name the three spies?

9 The three spies had two British helpers: can you name them?

10 Which playwright, author of *Private Lives*, reached 70 in 1969 and was knighted?

11 What post did Canada's Arnold Smith hold?

12 Whose radio diary came to an end in 1969?

13 Which artistic organization did Trevor Nunn head in 1968?

14 A scholar, yet blind and deaf from birth, this remarkable woman died in 1968. Her name?

15 Which Malcolm was famous as a writer, broadcaster and a critic of modern life?

. . . .

ANSWERS

1, Richard Nixon's 2, 1962 3, His brother John's 4, Francis Gary Powers 5, Rudolf Abel 6, The Soviet Union 7, The Portland ring 8, Peter and Helen Kroger, Gordon Lonsdale 9, Harry Houghton and Ethel Gee 10, Noel Coward 11, Secretary General of the Commonwealth 12, Mrs Dale's 13 The Royal Shakespeare Company 14, Helen Keller 15, Muggeridge

QUIZ 28
SPORT

. . . .

1 Which London soccer club had twins named Morgan in their end-of-60s team?

2 Which New Zealander set a new world record for the mile in 1962?

3 Were the 1962 World Cup soccer finals staged in Brazil, Chile or Argentina?

4 How many British teams qualified for the 1962 World Cup finals?

5 Mike Hailwood turned to Grand Prix racing after success as a) disc jockey b) motorcycle racer or c) soccer player?

6 Who became the youngest-ever Grand Prix motor racing world champion in 1963?

7 In which Olympics did Muhammad Ali win a gold medal?

8 Which British woman swimmer struck gold in the 1962 European championships?

9 Where were the 1968 Olympic Games held?

10 What was the nationality of 60s racing driver Jack Brabham?

11 In which event did Dick Fosbury famously "flop"?

12 An American driver won the 1961 Grand Prix world championship. Was he a) Dan Gurney b) Richie Ginther or c) Phil Hill?

13 Emile Griffith and Benny Paret were both 60s world champions; in which sport?

14 What nationality was Benny Paret?

15 What year did the US and Wimbledon tennis championships become "open"?

. . . .

ANSWERS

QUIZ 29
POT LUCK

. . . .

1   In what activity did Vidal Sassoon make his name?

2   Which British coin ceased to be legal tender in 1960?

3   What year was the Aberfan disaster in South Wales?

4   What year was Britain's first credit card introduced?

5   Why was Red Alligator in the news in 1968?

6   Who were the last to be called up in 1960?

7   Peter Dawson died in 1960; was he a) a singer b) a comedian
    c) a cricketer?

8   And was he a) Scottish b) Irish or c) Australian?

9   Hardy Amies designed what for the Queen: a) clothes b) gardens
    c) yachts?

10 What local government was replaced by the GLC?

11 What did GLC stand for?

12 Which skinny model became a fashion icon in 1967?

13 Which UN agency was awarded the Nobel peace prize in 1965?

14 Which three countries signed the 1963 nuclear test ban treaty?

15 Was Mary Quant associated with a) fashion, b) feminism, or c) sport?

. . . .

ANSWERS

1, Hairdressing 2, The farthing 3, 1966 4, 1966 5, It won the Grand National horse race 6, National servicemen 7, a) A singer 8, c) Australian 9, a) Clothes 10, The old London County Council 11, Greater London Council 12, Twiggy 13, United Nations Children's Fund (UNICEF) 14, USA, USSR, UK 15, a) Fashion

QUIZ 30
ARTS &
ENTERTAINMENT

· ·

1 Which historian wrote *The Collapse of the Third Republic*?

2 Which country was it about?

3 About which country had Shirer written an earlier and famous history?

4 Who wrote *Slaughterhouse-Five*?

5 What did the initials TWTWTW mean to British TV viewers from 1962?

6 Who made his name on the show and went on to achieve stardom as an interviewer and presenter?

7 Who was the show's resident singer?

8 Which of these was not a TWTWTW regular: Lance Percival, Willie Rushton, Peter Sellers?

9 What was the name of Harry H Corbett's character in the *Steptoe and Son* television series?

10 What was the name of his father?

11 What business were the pair in?

12 In which British TV show did the character Ena Sharpes appear?

13 Name the character in this show played by Pat Phoenix.

14 What was the third Bond movie?

15 Who played Pussy Galore in this film?

· ·

ANSWERS

1, William L Shirer 2, France 3, Nazi Germany 4, Kurt Vonnegut Jr 5, *That Was The Week That Was* 6, David Frost 7, Millicent Martin 8, Peter Sellers 9, Harold 10, Albert 11, Rag and bone men 12, *Coronation Street* 13, Elsie Tanner 14, *Goldfinger* 15, Honor Blackman

QUIZ 31
WORLD EVENTS

. . . .

1 What happened in the Ambassador Hotel, Los Angeles on June 6 1968?

2 Where was Camp David?

3 Who used it for top level meetings?

4 Where was Hamburger Hill?

5 What year was hanging abolished in Britain?

6 Who became Israel's first woman prime minister in 1969?

7 Of which African country was Haile Selassie the ruler?

8 In which country did President Novotny resign in 1968?

9 Of which country was Keith Holyoake prime minister in the 60s?

10 Who was elected US President as a result of the 1968 election?

11 Which spacecraft circled the Moon at Christmas 1968?

12 Who was the leader of Cyprus in 1960?

13 Who resigned as Israel's prime minister in January 1961?

14 Which African country was led by Jomo Kenyatta?

15 Which country did Warsaw Pact troops invade in August 1968?

. . . .

ANSWERS

1, Bobby Kennedy was shot 2, Maryland, USA 3, The President of the United States 4, Vietnam 5, 1969 6, Golda Meir 7, Ethiopia 8, Czechoslovakia 9, New Zealand 10, Richard M Nixon 11, "Apollo 8" 12, Archbishop Makarios 13, David Ben-Gurion 14, Kenya 15, Czechoslovakia

QUIZ 32
SPORT

. . . .

1 Which Spanish player took the 1965 US men's singles tennis title?

2 England soccer star Johnny Haynes played all his club football with one club: which one?

3 Which comedian was the club chairman?

4 Which British athlete won long jump gold at Tokyo in 1964?

5 She later married an American decathlete; his name?

6 The 1968 US women's singles tennis champion was British: was she a) Ann Jones b) Virginia Wade or c) Christine Truman?

7 Was Innes Ireland a 60s racing driver, jockey or baseball star?

8 Who was world champion on both two wheels and four?

9 What year did he add the Grand Prix drivers' title to earlier motorcycle championships?

10 Was soccer striker Ron Davies capped for Wales, England or Scotland in the 60s?

11 In 1968 Australia beat France in a World Cup final: in which sport?

12 Which US athlete held the world mile record from 1966 to 1975?

13 Whose 1968 long jump astonished everyone in Mexico City?

14 Why were performances at the Mexico City Olympics of 1968 both startling and controversial?

15 Which Italian tennis player won the 1960 French men's singles?

. . . .

ANSWERS

1, Manuel Santana 2, Fulham 3, Tommy Trinder 4, Mary Rand 5, Bill Toomey 6, b) Virginia Wade 7, Racing driver 8, John Surtees 9, 1964 10, Wales 11, Rugby League 12, Jim Ryun 13, Bob Beamon (who shattered the world record) 14, The Games were held at high altitude, producing some unusually fast times and long jumps 15, Nicola Pietrangeli

QUIZ 33
PEOPLE
1969

● ●

1 Of which country was V V Giri president in 1969?

2 Who became West German Chancellor in 1969?

3 Frank Duryea, who died in 1960, was an American pioneer of … what?

4 Which island was ruled by Dame Sibyl Hathaway?

5 Which organization was headed by General Lyman L Lemnitzer until 1969?

6 Thor Heyerdahl wrote a book about his most famous journey – called?

7 What did he call his 1969 reed boat?

8 Whose voyages was he attempting to recreate?

9 Who was re-elected Mayor of New York City in 1969?

10 Which well-known writer had tried, but failed, to get the same job?

11 Which publisher built up Pergamon Press, then lost it?

12 Which Beatle was rumoured to be dead in 1969, based on "clues" in songs and an album cover?

13 What sport was graced by Walter Hagen, who died in 1969?

14 A whiskery sidekick in Hopalong Cassidy westerns died in 1969; who was he?

15 He led the Boilermakers' Union in the UK; died in 1969. Who was he?

● ●

ANSWERS

QUIZ 34
POT LUCK

. . . .

1 Who recorded a song called *Love Me Do* in 1962?

2 Was Brian Kidd a) a pop singer b) a soccer player c) prime minister of New Zealand?

3 Jean Shrimpton was a famous 60s … a)singer b) model c) film star?

4 Why was James Meredith turned away from university in 1962?

5 Was *The Monster Mash* of 1962 a hit song, a food craze, or a giant earth-mover?

6 What was unusual about the Whiskey A-Go-Go of 1963?

7 Among its attractions were a) dancers in cages, b) lap dancers c) girls jumping out of giant bottles?

8 He was Shane Fenton in the 60s; by what name was he better known in the 70s?

9 Which Scottish loch was in the news when US nuclear submarines were based there?

10 Which pop singer became father to a daughter named Kim in 1960?

11 For which English club did John Atyeo play soccer?

12 What new form of car test was introduced in the UK in 1960?

13 Which composer's story was told in the film *Song Without End*?

14 All the rest in London in 1969 were red; but not this number 11. What was it?

15 Who met for the 200th time at Lord's in 1968?

. . . .

ANSWERS

1, The Beatles 2, b) he played for Man Utd 3, b) Model 4, He was a black student seeking admission to a segregated college in Mississippi, USA 5, "A song, by Bobby "Boris" Pickett and The Crypt-kickers 6, First disco on Los Angeles' Sunset Boulevard 7, a) Dancers in cages 8, Alvin Stardust 9, Holy Loch 10, Marty Wilde 11, Bristol City 12, The MOT 13, Franz Liszt 14, A London Transport bus, the first to be painted in advertising livery 15, England and Australia, at cricket

QUIZ 35
WORLD EVENTS

• •

1 Which British colony declared unilateral independence in 1965?
2 Where did US Marines land in 1965, at the start of a long war?
3 Who was chosen to lead the British Conservative Party in 1965?
4 Whom did he succeed?
5 Who was Prime Minister at the time of this change?
6 What tumultous event began in China in 1966?
7 Which woman became prime minister of India in 1966?
8 Of which country did Leonid Brezhnev become supreme leader in 1966?
9 Which war ended on 10 June 1967?
10 In which country was the Sharpeville massacre of 1960?
11 Which city was divided by a wall in 1961?
12 Who built it?
13 To which office was Michael Ramsey appointed in 1961?
14 Where was the Bay of Pigs?
15 And who landed there in 1961?

• •

ANSWERS

1, Rhodesia 2, Vietnam 3, Edward Heath 4, Alec Douglas-Home 5, Harold Wilson 6, The Cultural Revolution 7, Indira Gandhi 8, The Soviet Union 9, The Six-Day War in the Middle East 10, South Africa 11, Berlin 12, The East Germans 13, Archbishop of Canterbury 14, Cuba 15, Anti-Castro forces backed by the USA

QUIZ 36
PEOPLE

. . . .

1 Who wrote the song *Step Inside Love*?
2 And who sang it on her own TV show?
3 Which dj welcomed his radio audience with "Greetings, pop pickers"?
4 And the name of the show?
5 Where was Mariano Rumor prime minister in 1969?
6 Who sang The Times They Are A-Changin'?
7 Willy Ley died in 1969; about what had he written prophetically?
8 Sonja Henie, who died in 1969, was famous in which sport?
9 She later went on to success as a) a film star b) politician?
10 What country was she born in?
11 What was the surname of the popular singer Clodagh…?
12 Who were Reggie and Ronnie in London's underworld?
13 From which part of the British Isles did the pop group Marmalade originate?
14 Eric Portman died in 1969; was he a) an actor, b) a sportsman or c) a composer?
15 Who wrote *Ring of Bright Water*?

. . . .

ANSWERS

1, Paul McCartney 2, Cilla Black 3, Alan Freeman 4, *Pick of the Pops* 5, Italy 6, Bob Dylan 7, Space travel 8, Ice skating 9, a) A film star 10, Norway 11, Rogers 12, The Kray twins 13, Scotland 14, a) an actor 15, Gavin Maxwell

QUIZ 37
SPORT

. . . .

1 Which player won the Australian men's singles every year from 1963 to 1967?

2 In which events did America's Tommie Smith hold two world records?

3 What nationality was runner Herb Eliott?

4 A Mexican won the 1963 US men's singles tennis championship; who was he?

5 Was racing driver Denny Hulme a) a New Zealander b) Scottish c) South African?

6 At which weight did Howard Winstone win a world boxing title in 1968?

7 What was the nationality of 1963 world flyweight boxing champion Pone Kingpetch?

8 Mickey Mantle retired in 1969; which sport had he graced?

9 A French player won the 1967 French women's singles tennis title. Name?

10 An Australian girl won two French singles titles (1963 and 1965). Who was she?

11 Did John Newcombe of Australia ever win both US and Wimbledon titles in the same year?

12 Was the "Spirit of America" (1964) a) a spacecraft b) a land speed record holder or c) a balloon?

13 Which race was won in 1961, 1964 and 1967 by A J Foyt?

14 Which soccer striker moved from Aston Villa to Inter Milan in 1961?

15 Which Welsh international soccer star returned to Leeds from Juventus in 1962?

. . . .

ANSWERS

1, Roy Emerson 2, 200m and 400m 3, Australian 4, Rafael Osuna 5, a) A New Zealander 6, Featherweight 7, Thai 8, Baseball 9, François Durr 10, Lesley Turner 11, Yes, 1967 12, b) A land speed record holder 13, The Indianapolis 500 14, Gerry Hitchens 15, John Charles

QUIZ 38
PEOPLE

. . . .

1 For what was Jack Payne celebrated: a) leading a band or b) leading strikes?

2 Who wrote an autobiography called *Owning Up*?

3 What was Spiro Agnew's middle name?

4 Who lost his title to Muhammad Ali in 1964?

5 Where was the fight?

6 How many rounds did Liston last?

7 Name one (or all) of the three Bachelors

8 Which city did they come from?

9 Who played keyboards with the Animals before going off on his own?

10 Who was married to Cher?

11 And what was their 1965 hit song?

12 What was Cilla Black's real name?

13 Can you name her first big hit?

14 This song was also recorded by an American. Who?

15 Which American-born poet died in London in 1965?

. . . .

ANSWERS

WORLD EVENTS
1963

• •

1 Which British politician was at the centre of a 1963 sex scandal?

2 Which two young women became front-page news for their part in this affair?

3 Which European city did President Kennedy make an historic visit to in 1963?

4 What did Britain agree to buy from the USA in 1963 to boost its defences?

5 Whose disappearance in 1963 sparked rumours of a spy scandal?

6 The man described as the "architect of the Welfare State" died in March 1963. His name?

7 Whose 1963 report led to wholesale closures of Britain's railway lines?

8 Which unusual crime made British headlines in August 1963?

9 How much was stolen in that crime: a) half a million pounds, b) two and a half million, c) ten million?

10 Which religious leader died in June 1963?

11 Which European city was devastated by a 1963 earthquake?

12 Who said "I have a dream" in Washington in 1963?

13 Whose murder took place on 30 November 1963?

14 Who was arrested on suspicion of having committed the murder?

15 Who then shot the arrested suspect?

• •

ANSWERS

1, John Profumo 2, Christine Keeler and Mandy Rice-Davies 3, Berlin 4, Polaris missiles 5, Kim Philby 6, Lord Beveridge 7, Lord Beeching 8, The Great Train Robbery 9, b) £2½ million 10, Pope John XXIII 11, Skopje 12, Martin Luther King 13, John F Kennedy 14, Lee Harvey Oswald 15, Jack Ruby

QUIZ 40
ARTS & ENTERTAINMENT

- -

1 For which 1964 role did Julie Andrews win an Oscar?

2 Who wrote the book on which the film was based?

3 Which American actor played Bert with a Cockney accent in the film?

4 Who wrote the novel on which *The Carpetbaggers* was based?

5 Who starred as Eliza in the film of *My Fair Lady*?

6 Which actor played Professor Higgins in *My Fair Lady* on film and on stage?

7 Which veteran actor starred as the dustman Doolittle?

8 Was the main character in TV's *Ironside* confined to a wheelchair, blind, or partly bionic?

9 And was he a detective, a doctor, or a lawyer?

10 Who played Ironside?

11 Which courtroom role had this actor previously played on TV?

12 With which sport was commentator Kenneth Wolstenholme associated on British television?

13 Which up-and-coming tough guy starred in the TV Western *Rawhide* as Rowdy Yates?

14 Who were the two main stars of the film *Zulu*?

15 In which country was *Zulu* set?

- -

ANSWERS

1, Mary Poppins 2, P L Travers 3, Dick Van Dyke 4, Harold Robbins 5, Audrey Hepburn 6, Rex Harrison 7, Stanley Holloway 8, He was confined to a wheelchair 9, A detective 10, Raymond Burr 11, Perry Mason 12, Soccer 13, Clint Eastwood 14, Michael Caine and Stanley Baker 15, South Africa

QUIZ 41
PEOPLE

. . . .

1 Which songwriters penned *Trains and Boats and Planes*?

2 Who partnered Peter in a singing duo?

3 Who was Peter's sister?

4 And whose girlfriend was she for a time?

5 Who was the lead singer of The Four Pennies?

6 He was married to an actress; who?

7 Who was the Rolling Stones' drummer (still going strong)?

8 Which magazines did Henry Luce (died 1967) found?

9 Which 60s singer fronted the Blue Flames?

10 Who were Florence, Mary and Diana?

11 Thomas Jones Woodward became a star as …?

12 Which pantomime role did Cliff Richard take on in 1964-65: a) Puss in Boots b) Aladdin or c) Dick Whittington?

13 She partnered Nelson Eddy, and she died in 1965. Who was she?

14 What instrument did Jack Teagarden play?

15 Who received a record jail term for spying in May 1961?

. . . .

ANSWERS

1, Burt Bacharach and Hal David 2, Gordon 3, Jane Asher 4, Paul McCartney's 5, Lionel Morton 6, Julia Foster 7, Charlie Watts 8, *Time* and *Life* 9, Georgie Fame 10, The Supremes 11, Tom Jones 12, b) Aladdin 13, Jeanette MacDonald 14, Trombone 15, George Blake

POT LUCK

• •

1 Which Scottish actor made the headlines as Hamlet in 1969?

2 Which US city elected the same mayor three times in the 60s?

3 Who was the mayor?

4 Which corporation did Lee Iacocca head for a time?

5 Whom did Princess Sophia of Greece marry?

6 Of which country was Simon Kapepwe vice-president?

7 Who succeeded Michael Stewart as British Foreign Secretary in 1966?

8 What did the US lose over the Atlantic in 1966?

9 What first did Edward Brooke achieve in 1966?

10 What did France pull out of in 1966?

11 Who received a posthumous pardon in 1966 for murders thought to have been committed by John Reginald Christie?

12 In which country was Rudi Dutschke famous?

13 As what?

14 Which two British banks merged in 1968?

15 To form?

• •

ANSWERS

1, Nicol Williamson. 2, New York City. 3, Sam Yorty. 4, Ford Motor Co. 5, Prince Juan Carlos of Spain. 6, Zambia. 7, George Brown. 8, A nuclear bomb. 9, He was the first black US senator. 10, NATO. 11, Timothy Evans. 12, Germany. 13, A student protest leader. 14, National Provincial and Westminster. 15, NatWest

QUIZ 43
ARTS & ENTERTAINMENT

1 Was *Z-Cars* a British tv series about police, paramedics or racing drivers?

2 Who played Barlow in the series?

3 What was the name of his long-suffering colleague, played by Frank Windsor?

4 Another character called Smith had a nickname: what was it?

5 And who played him?

6 What was the Beatles' first film?

7 Who directed the film and when was it released?

8 Who starred alongside Jane Fonda in *Cat Ballou*?

9 Who was the star of *The Ipcress File*?

10 The English half of the most famous film comedy pair died in 1965; who was he?

11 Which London theatre, famed for its statuesque nudes, closed in 1964?

12 Which Shakespeare role did Laurence Olivier release on screen in 1965?

13 What was the title of the first live pop show on British commercial televison, launched in 1964?

14 Was John Arlott famous for radio commentaries on boxing, cricket, or tennis?

15 Who wrote the scripts for Tony Hancock's TV shows?

ANSWERS

1, Police 2, Stratford Johns 3, John Watt 4, Fancy 5, Brian Blessed 6, A *Hard Day's Night* 7, Richard Lester, 1963 8, Lee Marvin 9, Michael Caine 10, Stan Laurel 11, The Windmill 12, Othello 13, *Ready, Steady, Go!* 14, Cricket 15, Alan Simpson and Ray Galton

QUIZ 44
WORLD EVENTS

. . . .

1 To which Mediterranean island were UN peacekeepers sent in 1964?

2 The PLO was formed in 1964; what do the initials stand for?

3 Chad became independent in 1960 – which European country had governed it?

4 Which fiery Welsh Labour MP and builder of the National Health Service died in 1960?

5 What was his wife's name – she was also a politician?

6 Albert Kesselring died in 1960; in which war had he been a general?

7 On which side?

8 Which US leader's son died 36 hours after birth in 1963?

9 What did a British doctor state in 1963 would never be possible?

10 Where did Russian troops block US trucks in 1963?

11 Which country was banned from the Olympics in 1964?

12 Which two countries were the major aid suppliers to North Vietnam?

13 Which Eastern bloc military organization opposed NATO in Europe?

14 What year was the "Prague spring"

15 In which country was the Biafran war?

. . . .

ANSWERS

1, Cyprus 2, Palestine Liberation Organization 3, France 4, Aneurin Bevan 5, Jennie Lee 6, World War II 7, Germany 8, Kennedy's 9, Sex change operations 10, On their way to West Berlin 11, South Africa 12, USSR and China 13, The Warsaw Pact 14, 1968 15, Nigeria

POT LUCK

1960

. . . .

1 Of which state was Marshal Voroshilov head of state in 1960?

2 Which African dam was opened in 1960 by the Queen Mother?

3 On which river was it built?

4 What was a Sunday sporting "first" in Britain in 1960?

5 Which pop singer said goodbye to the US Army in 1960?

6 What was the U-2?

7 What happened to Gary Powers' U-2?

8 Which singing duo told little Susie to wake up?

9 Which classic British car make ceased production in 1960?

10 At what did Patterson beat Johansson?

11 Which state did Senator John F Kennedy represent in 1960?

12 Who was campaign manager for his presidential campaign?

13 What was the *France* which took to the water in 1960?

14 Which country caused protests by testing nuclear weapons in 1960?

15 What disease was found to be on the increase among US teenagers in 1960?

. . . .

ANSWERS

1, Soviet Union 2, Kariba Dam 3, Zambezi 4, Professional soccer 5, Elvis Presley 6, A US spy plane 7, It was shot down by Soviet air defences 8, The Everly Brothers 9, Armstrong Siddeley 10, Boxing (Floyd Patterson beat Ingemar Johansson for the world heavyweight title) 11, Massachusetts 12, His brother Robert F Kennedy 13, The world's longest ocean liner 14, France 15, Venereal disease

PEOPLE

. . . .

1 Wayne Gretzky was born in 1961 in Canada; in which sport did he become a star?

2 Who was Jan Palach?

3 Sir Francis Chichester was knighted in 1967. Where did the ceremony take place?

4 In what activity did Sir Victor Gollancz (died 1967) engage?

5 Known as "the last of the red-hot mamas", she died in 1966. Who was she?

6 Which smooth-voiced American singer died in February 1965?

7 Which British actor-knight died the same month?

8 Where was Prince Andrew born?

9 And in which year?

10 What did Chester Nimitz (died 1966) have named after him?

11 In which campaigns had Nimitz distinguished himself?

12 What fate befell Malcolm X in 1965?

13 Where?

14 What was Malcom X's original name?

15 Of which group was Malcolm X a leader?

. . . .

ANSWERS

1, Ice hockey 2, A Czech student who burned himself to death in protest at Soviet actions 3, Greenwich 4, Publishing 5, Sophie Tucker 6, Nat "King" Cole 7, Sir Donald Wolfit 8, Buckingham Palace 9, 1960 10, A class of US aircraft carriers 11, The Pacific sea battles of World War II 12, He was murdered 13, New York City 14, Malcolm Little 15, The Black Muslims

QUIZ 47
ARTS & ENTERTAINMENT

1 Which battered-featured actor partnered Tony Hancock in many radio and TV shows?

2 With which comedy film series was he also famously associated?

3 Another star of the same series appeared on radio's *Round the Horne*? Who was he?

4 Which catch-phrase did he use on radio with Tony Hancock?

5 In which artform was Roger McGough famous: poetry, dance or music?

6 *Door into the Dark* was a 1969 collection from which Irish poet?

7 Who wrote *The Bell Jar* (1963)?

8 What happened to her that same year?

9 Who was her poet-husband?

10 Can you complete this 60s film title: *Bunny Lake is* …?

11 Still going strong in the 60s, who played Sgt Ernie Bilko on television?

12 Which British TV policeman plodded the beat around Dock Green?

13 Who played Dr Zhivago on screen?

14 Who was the author of the book on which the film was based?

15 Which American "beat-poet" died in 1969?

ANSWERS

QUIZ 48
PEOPLE

. . . .

1 Where did Kwame Nkrumah seek refuge in 1966?

2 Who had overthrown him?

3 And which country had he ruled until his overthrow?

4 With which political party was Herbert Morrison (died 1965) associated?

5 What year did singer Nelson Eddy die?

6 What year was Prince Edward born?

7 What were his full first names?

8 Jimmy Wilde (died 1969) had been a world champion ... what?

9 Which of the three "Ws" of West Indian cricket died in 1967?

10 Who were the two crewmen of the US "Gemini 8" spacecraft (1966)?

11 Which islanders began going home from Britain in 1963?

12 Why had they had to leave?

13 Which ex-king of Egypt died in 1965?

14 When had he lost his throne?

15 The author of *The Quare Fellow* died in Dublin in 1964; who was he?

. . . .

ANSWERS

1, Guinea 2, The army 3, Ghana 4, Labour 5, 1967 6, 1964 7, Edward Antony
Richard Louis 8, Boxer 9, Sir Frank Worrell 10, Neil Armstrong and David Scott
11, Tristan da Cunha's 12, They had to be evacuated after a volcano erupted in
1961 13, Farouk 14, 1952 15, Brendan Behan

SPORT

. . . .

1 Ted Williams and Casey Stengel were elected to this sport's Hall of Fame in 1966. The sport?

2 What did Weatherly beat Gretel to win in 1962?

3 What was Ralph Boston's star event on the track?

4 Which Scottish swimmer set a world 100-yard record in 1966?

5 Which London soccer team shortened its name for the 67–68 season?

6 For which London soccer side did the Harris brothers, Ron and Alan, play in the 60s?

7 Which man won the tennis Grand Slam (all four major titles) in 1969?

8 Which baseball team scored a record 240 home runs in 1961?

9 Which team won baseball's World Series in 1961 and 1962?

10 What nationality was cyclist Eddy Merckx?

11 What year did he first win the Tour de France?

12 In which sport was Joe Namath a star?

13 Which team did he play for in the 1969 season?

14 Which Welsh rugby player scored a record 19 points on his debut in 1967?

15 Which Phil captained England's rugby team in 1967?

. . . .

ANSWERS

1, Baseball 2, The America's Cup (yacht race) 3, Long jump 4, Bobby McGregor 5, Leyton Orient, to Orient 6, Chelsea 7, Rod Laver 8, New York Yankees 9, New York Yankees 10, Belgian 11, 1969 12, American football 13, The New York Jets 14, Keith Jarrett 15, Phil Judd

QUIZ 50
PEOPLE

. . . .

1 Whom did Henry Cooper beat in 1961 to win a Lonsdale belt?

2 He died in 1966, he wrote the "Hornblower" stories. Who was he?

3 What did his initials stand for?

4 Which famous American general died in April 1964?

5 The author of *Brideshead Revisited* died in 1966. His name?

6 Where was Adolf Eichmann put on trial?

7 How many times did Yuri Gagarin circle the Earth in 1961?

8 What did Gary Kasparov (born 1963) grow up to be good at?

9 Which German statesman died in April 1967?

10 When had he held power as Chancellor of West Germany?

11 Which Canadian political party did Pierre Trudeau lead?

12 Which European king had to flee in 1967 after an army coup?

13 Of which country was Sir Walter Nash, who died in 1968, prime minister?

14 Which busty American actress died in a 1967 car crash?

15 Who became leader of the PLO in 1969?

. . . .

ANSWERS

1, Joe Erskine 2, C S Forester 3, Cecil Scott 4, Douglas MacArthur 5, Evelyn Waugh 6, Jerusalem 7, Once 8, Chess 9, Konrad Adenauer 10, 1949 to 1963 11, The Liberal Party 12, Constantine II of Greece 13, New Zealand 14, Jayne Mansfield 15, Yasser Arafat

QUIZ 51
ART & ENTERTAINMENT

1 Famous for his books on "one-upmanship", died in 1969; who was he?

2 What part did Christopher Plummer play in the film *The Sound of Music?*

3 Who sang the title song?

4 Which historical figure was the focus for *A Man For All Seasons*?

5 Who wrote the play?

6 Who played the leading role in the film?

7 In which 60s film did Charlton Heston play General Gordon?

8 What year did Buster Keaton die?

9 Which Soviet writer defected to the West in 1969?

10 Who was the famous wife of Desi Arnaz?

11 Which part of her anatomy did the witch in TV's Bewitched wiggle to make magic?

12 Who played this witch?

13 Whose poem "Babi Yar" (1963) made him famous outside the Soviet Union?

14 Which country produced in 1966 "the best ever" film of Shakespeare's *Hamlet?*

15 What was the title of Clint Eastwood's first "spaghetti Western" (1964)?

ANSWERS

1, Stephen Potter. 2, Captain Von Trapp 3, Julie Andrews 4, Sir Thomas More 5, Robert Bolt 6, Paul Scofield 7, *Khartoum* 8, 1966 9, Anatoli Kuznetsov 10, Lucille Ball 11, Her nose 12, Elizabeth Montgomery 13, Yevgeny Yevtushenko 14, The USSR 15, *A Fistful of Dollars*

QUIZ 52

POT LUCK

1960

. . . .

1 Which racing driver won the 1960 Monaco Grand Prix, and lost his driving licence the same year?

2 Which African state was hit by a disastrous earthquake in 1960?

3 Which short-lived American mail service was remembered in 1960, its 200th anniversary?

4 Which American politician spoke of a "New Frontier"?

5 Who captained the Wolverhampton Wanderers team that won the FA Cup?

6 Where were the TT races held?

7 What appeared for the first time at the May Day parade in Moscow?

8 Which mountain did the Chinese claim to have climbed by the north face?

9 Which visiting statesman told journalists he was "off on a pub crawl"?

10 In which city was he?

11 What was significant in the list of new cardinals (March 1960)?

12 Where were the 1960 Olympic Games held?

13 What was a Kenwood Chef?

14 Who was king of Belgium and cut short his honeymoon because of troubles at home?

15 Which famous actor-couple were divorced in December 1960?

. . . .

ANSWERS

1, Stirling Moss 2, Morocco 3, The Pony Express 4, John F Kennedy 5, Bill Slater 6, The Isle of Man 7, Missiles 8, Everest 9, Harold Macmillan 10, Paris 11, The first black African cardinals were appointed 12, Rome 13, A food mixer 14, Baudouin 15, Laurence Olivier and Vivien Leigh

QUIZ 53
PEOPLE

. . . .

1 In which country was Lord Beaverbrook born?

2 With which British newspaper was he most famously associated?

3 What was his "common" name?

4 What year did he die?

5 For what was Primo Carnera (died 1967) famous?

6 Who was born at Park House, Sandringham on 1 July 1960?

7 For which county did Walter Hammond (died 1965) play cricket?

8 Who sailed round the world in Lively Lady?

9 The author of *The Sound and the Fury* died in 1962: who was he?

10 Was he American, British or Australian?

11 Of which country was Dr Banda president?

12 What was his first name?

13 What sport did Bill Woodfull (died 1965) play?

14 Who presented television's *What's My Line* until 1963?

15 What was the professional name of Julie Elizabeth Webb?

. . . .

ANSWERS

1, Canada 2, *The Daily Express* 3, Max Aitken 4, 1964 5, Italian boxer, world champion 1933-34 6, Princess Diana 7, Gloucestershire 8, Alec Rose 9, William Faulkner 10, American 11, Malawi 12, Hastings 13, Cricket, for Australia 14, Eamonn Andrews 15, Julie Andrews

QUIZ 54
POT LUCK

. . . .

1 What was the 1964 Fastback project designed to produce?

2 How many people watched the Apollo Moon landing on TV in 1969?

3 Which Canadian tried to buy *The Times* newspaper?

4 Which was the first BBC local radio station?

5 What year did it open?

6 Which Welsh town became a city in 1969?

7 In which city did Jack Ruby die in 1967?

8 Who was killed on Coniston Water in 1967?

9 What was he doing?

10 What did Stamford Brook Tube station in London have in 1964 that was unique?

11 Who became the first Pope to visit the Holy Land, in 1964?

12 Calvin Smith was born in 1961; in which sport did he achieve fame?

13 Which famous snooker champion was born on 13 January 1969 in Scotland?

14 What year did NHS prescriptions become free of charge?

15 When were charges re-introduced?

. . . .

ANSWERS

1, A new breed of pig 2, 600 million 3, Lord Roy Thompson of Fleet (in 1966) 4, Radio Leicester 5, 1967 6, Swansea 7, Dallas 8, Donald Campbell 9, Trying to break his own water speed record 10, London's first automatic ticket barrier 11, Paul VI 12, Athletics 13, Stephen Hendry 14, 1965 15, 1968

QUIZ 55
SPORT

. . . .

1 What was tennis star Rod Laver's middle name?

2 Professional baseball in the USA celebrated its centenary; in which year?

3 In which sport was Alun Pask a 60s Welsh star?

4 Did Scotland's Jim Baxter play soccer, golf or cricket?

5 In which sport was Nigeria's Dick Tiger a double world champion?

6 Who was Britain's only world middleweight boxing champion in the 1960s?

7 In which sport was France's Jacques Anquetil a 60s star?

8 Camberabero and Spanghero were familiar names to fans of which sport in the late 60s?

9 For which national side did these two play?

10 Which of these1967–68 soccer clubs are still in the Football League: Workington, Barrow, Stockport?

11 A baseball team founded in 1962 won the 1969 World Series; who were they?

12 Who hit his 600th home run in 1969 to equal a baseball record?

13 Whose record had he matched?

14 Which London team did Jimmy Greaves sign for in 1961?

15 From which overseas club was he transferred?

. . . .

ANSWERS

1, George 2, 1969 3, Rugby union 4, Soccer 5, Boxing (world middleweight and light-heavyweight champion) 6, Terry Downes 7, Cycling (especially the Tour de France) 8, Rugby Union 9, France 10, Stockport 11, The New York Mets 12, Willie Mays 13, Babe Ruth's 14, Tottenham Hotspur 15, Milan

QUIZ 56
PEOPLE

. . . .

1 Which novelist wrote a new James Bond novel in 1968?

2 What was the title?

3 In which film did his teenage son (later also a novelist) appear in 1965?

4 Which former Labour prime minister died in 1967?

5 Which former prime minister became the Earl of Avon in 1961?

6 Who gave up a title in 1963 to be an MP?

7 What was his title?

8 Who climbed Annapurna II in 1960?

9 Who wrote *Life at the Top*?

10 To which book was it a sequel?

11 Which actor, famous in the 90s, was born in Belfast in 1960?

12 Which Yorkshire cricketer made his England debut in 1964?

13 How old was Richard Branson in 1960?

14 Which New Zealander was 1964 world speedway champion?

15 Who was to be found riding a horse called Mister Softee?

. . . .

ANSWERS

1, Kingsley Amis 2, *Colonel Sun* 3, *A High Wind in Jamaica* 4, Clement Attlee 5, Sir Anthony Eden 6, Tony Benn 7, Viscount Stansgate 8, Chris Bonington 9, John Braine 10, *Room at the Top* 11, Kenneth Branagh 12, Geoff Boycott 13, Ten 14, Barry Briggs 15, David Broome

QUIZ 57
POT LUCK

. . . .

1 Which mild-mannered horror-film actor died in 1969?

2 Which was the first British newspaper to issue a colour supplement?

3 When?

4 Which mountain's north face was climbed in winter for the first time in 1962?

5 Which Sunday newspaper appeared for the first time in 1962?

6 Where were the 1968 Winter Olympics held?

7 Which new arena opened in New York City in 1968?

8 On which planet did the Russians land a probe in 1966?

9 What sport did Wilt Chamberlain play?

10 What record did he achieve in 1960?

11 Which British javelin thrower was born in 1961?

12 Which Czech tennis star was born in March 1960?

13 Which London Tube line opened in 1969?

14 Which Indian Ocean island became independent in 1968?

15 What colour were the old £5 notes that ceased to be legal tender in Britain in 1961?

. . . .

ANSWERS

15, Black and white
11, Fatima Whitbread 12, Ivan Lendl 13, The Victoria Line 14, Mauritius
9, Basketball 10, He scored all his team's 100 points, playing for Philadelphia
Telegraph 6, Grenoble, France 7, The new Madison Square Garden 8, Venus
1, Boris Karloff 2, The Sunday Times 3, Feb 62 4, The Matterhorn 5, The Sunday

QUIZ 58
ARTS & ENTERTAINMENT

. . . .

1 Name the actors who played the men from UNCLE on TV and film.

2 What was the leading character called?

3 And his assistant?

4 Which Redgrave starred in *Georgy Girl*?

5 Which Redgrave starred in *Blow-Up*?

6 Which erotic bestseller of 1749 by John Cleland was republished in 1964?

7 Who starred as America's answer to James Bond in the 1966 movie *Our Man Flint*?

8 On whose stories was Disney's *The Jungle* Book based?

9 Bert Lahr died in 1967; which role was he famous for on screen?

10 Which London theatre opened in 1969: Greenwich, National, Lyceum?

11 Who wrote *The Son of Man*?

12 Complete this play title: *Play It …*

13 *Far From the Madding Crowd* was a 60s film version of a novel by… whom?

14 Name the co-stars of *In the Heat of the Night*?

15 Name the detective played by Poitier.

. . . .

ANSWERS

1, Robert Vaughn and David McCallum 2, Napoleon Solo 3, Ilya Kuryakin 4, Lynn 5, Vanessa 6, *Fanny Hill* 7, James Coburn 8, Rudyard Kipling 9, The Cowardly Lion in *The Wizard of Oz* 10, Greenwich Theatre 11, Dennis Potter 12, *Again, Sam* 13, Thomas Hardy 14, Rod Steiger and Sidney Poitier 15, Virgil Tibbs

QUIZ 59
PEOPLE

• •

1 Which newsreader became editor of the *Economist* magazine in 1964?

2 In which 1969 war film did Burton and Eastwood co-star?

3 Who became Britain's deputy prime minister in 1963?

4 By what name was he known to friends?

5 To whom had he lost a party leadership contest?

6 And in which party?

7 What was Maurice Micklewhite's screen name?

8 Which journalist presented a TV series called *Men Of Our Time* (1963)?

9 Which government post did James Callaghan take in 1967?

10 Which job had he held in the newly elected Labout government of 1964?

11 Which comedian wore a fez?

12 Who became Britain's new Minister of Technology in 1964?

13 In which sphere had he been active before entering the government?

14 Which character was created by Richmal Crompton, who died in 1969?

15 Was this author a man or a woman?

• •

ANSWERS

1. Alastair Burnett 2. *Where Eagles Dare* 3. R A Butler 4. Rab (from his initials) 5. Lord Home 6. The Conservative Party 7. Michael Caine 8. James Cameron 9. Home Secretary 10. Chancellor of the Exchequer 11. Tommy Cooper 12. Frank Cousins 13. Trade unionism (with the Transport and General Workers' Union) 14. William 15. A woman

QUIZ 60
ARTS & ENTERTAINMENT

· ·

1 Who wrote *The Valley of Bones* (1964)?

2 Which science fiction author wrote *The Machineries of Joy*?

3 Which sport featured in the novel and film *This Sporting Life*?

4 Who wrote the novel?

5 Who played the central character in the film version?

6 Who starred in the musical *Half a Sixpence*?

7 What was the title of Roy Dotrice's one-man show about diarist John Aubrey?

8 Who directed the 1967 film *A Countess from Hong Kong*?

9 Which Western veteran starred in *El Dorado* and *The War Wagon*?

10 Which Indian city figured in the title of a sensational stage show?

11 Complete the title of this Julie Andrews 60s film: *Thoroughly Modern …*?

12 What was the first James Bond movie?

13 Who played 007 in the first Bond film?

14 Which Robert went barefoot in the park in a film of the same title?

15 Which playwright wrote *Saved*?

· ·

ANSWERS

1, Anthony Powell 2, Ray Bradbury 3, Rugby League 4, David Storey 5, Richard Harris 6, Tommy Steele 7, *Brief Lives* 8, Charlie Chaplin 9, John Wayne 10, Calcutta (*Oh Calcutta!*) 11, Millie 12, *Dr No* 13, Sean Connery 14, Robert Redford 15, Edward Bond

QUIZ 61
SPORT
SOCCER

. . . .

1 Who was England soccer manager before Alf Ramsey?

2 What halted the 1962–63 soccer season in Britain a) bad weather b) a players' strike c) a bribery scandal?

3 Which ageing soccer star returned to his roots in 1961?

4 With which English soccer club did Scot Ian St John become a legend?

5 Did Rodney Marsh begin his soccer career with a) QPR b) Fulham or c) Man City?

6 For which 60s soccer club did Jimmy Adamson and Andy Lochhead play at Turf Moor?

7 Fred Pickering and Bryan Douglas played together at Ewood Park for … who in the 60s?

8 Eric Caldow played for which Scottish club?

9 For which team did Gary Sprake keep goal?

10 He went on to manage Arsenal and Spurs; in 1964 he was playing for Chelsea. Who is he?

11 Was Peter Rodrigues a 60s international for a) Spain b) Wales c) France?

12 How many Manchester United players were in the 1966 World Cup winning team?

13 For which soccer team did Peter Bonetti keep goal?

14 What was his nickname: a) The Monkey b) The Cat c) The Black Flash?

15 Was Cliff Jones a Welsh or Irish international soccer star?

. . . .

ANSWERS

1. Walter Winterbottom 2. a) Snow and ice 3. Stanley Matthews, who signed for Stoke City, his first club 4. Liverpool 5. b) Fulham 6. Burnley 7. Blackburn Rovers 8. Glasgow Rangers 9. Leeds United 10. George Graham 11. b) Wales 12. Two (Bobby Charlton and Nobby Stiles) 13. Chelsea 14. b) The Cat 15. Welsh

QUIZ 62
PEOPLE

. . . .

1 Viscount Cunningham, died 1963, was a famous: a) naval commander b) pilot c) ruler of India?

2 In which war had he gained fame?

3 Which Hull-born actor made his Old Vic debut in 1960?

4 Husband of actress Sybil Thorndike, he died in 1969: who was he?

5 Who was made Minister of Transport in 1965?

6 Why did her appointment cause some amusement among drivers?

7 Who created a TV character called E L Wisty?

8 How many rounds did boxer Henry Cooper last in his second fight with Cassius Clay (Muhammad Ali)?

9 Where did Robin Cook attend university in the 60s?

10 Which famous snooker player was awarded the OBE in 1963?

11 A player with the same surname later matched this player's fame. Who was he?

12 How old was he in 1963?

13 Who presented BBC TV's *Panorama* from 1967 to 72?

14 What his sartorial trademark?

15 For which party had he stood unsuccessfully as a candidate in the 1959 election?

. . . .

ANSWERS

QUIZ 63
POT LUCK

. . . .

1 Which famous US prison closed in 1963?

2 Where was it?

3 Actor Peter Lorre died in 1964; where was he born?

4 What did the D in Dwight D Eisenhower stand for?

5 What year did Eisenhower die?

6 How did the authorities get rid of the wrecked tanker "Torrey Canyon"?

7 What year was the "Torrey Canyon" disaster?

8 How many new boroughs were there in the new Greater London Council?

9 What was unusual about some London Tube trains in 1964?

10 Which country launched a satellite called "Early Bird"?

11 Where was the Astrodome, opened in 1965?

12 And what was it?

13 What was televised for the first time in 1966?

14 How many TV channels did Britain have from May 1964?

15 What were they?

. . . .

ANSWERS

1, Alcatraz 2, San Francisco Bay, California 3, Hungary 4, David 5, 1969 6, It was bombed 7, 1967 8, 32 plus the City of London 9, They had no drivers 10, The USA 11, Houston, Texas 12, The world's first completely roofed-over stadium 13, The opening of parliament in Britain 14, Three 15, BBC-1, ITV and the new addition, BBC-2

WORLD EVENTS
1961

. . . .

1 With whom did the US break off diplomatic relations?

2 What happened in Wandsworth and Maidstone jails?

3 Where did the Afro-Shirazi Party win elections?

4 Which British newspaper changed owners in January?

5 Who quit as Israel's prime minister?

6 Which Congolese politician was murdered?

7 Which airline's Boeing 707 crashed near Brussels?

8 Which country did the UN tell to reform its rule in Angola?

9 For what did Gordon Lonsdale go on trial in London?

10 What nationality was he (probably)?

11 Where did the British liner "Dara" catch fire?

12 What were found in a cave in Judaea?

13 Which organization for young people was set up in the USA?

14 Where did Ngo Dinh Diem win an election?

15 Which neighbouring state did Iraq lay claim to?

. . . .

ANSWERS

1. Cuba 2. The prisoners mutinied 3. Zanzibar 4. *The Daily Herald*
5. David Ben-Gurion 6. Patrice Lumumba 7. Sabena 8. Portugal 9. Spying
10. Russian 11. The Persian Gulf 12. 40 Biblical scrolls 13. The Peace Corps
14. South Vietnam 15. Kuwait

ARTS & ENTERTAINMENT

- -

1 In which film did Taylor play Katherine to Burton's Petruchio?

2 In a 1962 movie, Donald Pleasence played a murderer arrested in 1910; name the murderer.

3 Which naturalist wrote A *Zoo In My Luggage*?

4 His novelist brother wrote *Clea* (1960); the brother's name?

5 *Clea* was the fourth in a series of novels known as …?

6 Which Dickens' book became a 1967 musical hit on screen?

7 Which twinkletoed dancer was still going strong in *Finian's Rainbow*?

8 Complete the title of this 1966 Western: *The Good, the Bad and* …?

9 Who starred in the film as "the man with no name"?

10 Which British comedian starred as a bumbling bullfighter in a 1967 film called *The Bobo*?

11 Who wrote *Soul on Ice*, about black people in the United States?

12 Did the 1968 film *How to Steal the World* star a) the Men from UNCLE, b) James Bond, or c) The Saint?

13 Who emerged from the sea to look for shells in the first James Bond film?

14 Writer of 1500 songs including great hits from musicals such as *Guys and Dolls*; he died in 1969; who was he?

15 Who was the screen Barbarella?

- -

ANSWERS

QUIZ 66
SCIENCE & TECHNOLOGY

. . . .

1 How many times a minute did an LP record revolve?

2 What was the slightly faster speed of a single?

3 Who had a noise reduction system named after him in 1967?

4 What year did instant colour snaps become available?

5 From which manufacturer?

6 Who was the brains behind instant photos?

7 Whose animated fighting skeletons enlivened a 1963 film?

8 And the film?

9 At what London college was Denis Gabor working in 1967?

10 With which invention is he associated?

11 Of which diagnostic technique was obstetrician Ian Donald a pioneer?

12 By what name was the Sellafield nuclear plant known in the 60s?

13 With which kind of machinery was Harry Ferguson (died 1960) associated?

14 For what kind of photos was Eric Hosking famous?

15 What kind of craft was used to explore the Amazon in 1968?

. . . .

ANSWERS

1. 33 and a third 2. 45 rpm 3. Ray Dolby 4. 1963 5. Polaroid 6. Edwin H Land
7. Ray Harryhausen 8. *Jason and the Argonauts* 9. Imperial College
10. Holography 11. Ultrasound scans 12. Windscale 13. Tractors 14. Bird pictures
15. Hovercraft

QUIZ 67
ARTS & ENTERTAINMENT

. . . .

1 Whose first film as director was *Whistle Down The Wind* (1961)?

2 Who was his actress wife?

3 Who wrote *The L-Shaped Room*?

4 Which British poet wrote *Wodwo*?

5 Who appeared on screen with the animals as Dr Doolittle?

6 A movie great died on 12 June 1967; famous for his roles alongside Katherine Hepburn, he was …?

7 Died 8 July 1967, once married to Laurence Olivier, star of *Gone With the Wind*. Her name?

8 Who wrote *Why Are We in Vietnam*?

9 Who wrote *Something to Answer For* (1968)?

10 P H Newby won a new literary prize in 1969; which one?

11 What did the initials P H stand for?

12 Which undressed stage show did Michael Butler unveil in 1968?

13 Who were the co-stars of *Easy Rider*?

14 Which culture was the subject of the film *Alice's Restaurant*?

15 Who sang the title song from this film?

. . . .

ANSWERS

1, Bryan Forbes 2, Nanette Newman 3, Lynne Reid-Banks 4, Ted Hughes 5, Rex Harrison 6, Spencer Tracy 7, Vivien Leigh 8, Norman Mailer 9, P H Newby 10, The Booker Prize 11, Percy Howard 12, *Hair* 13, Peter Fonda and Dennis Hopper 14, Hippie 15, Arlo Guthrie

QUIZ 68
SPORT

. . . .

1 For which London club did Bill Brown keep goal?

2 Which English soccer team did Scotland's Pat Crerand play for?

3 Which Scottish club won the European Cup in 1967?

4 Who was their manager?

5 Whom did they beat in the European Cup final?

6 And what was the score?

7 Who scored for Celtic?

8 Which was the next British team to win the European Cup?

9 When?

10 Who was their manager?

11 Two brothers each won the Footballer of the Year title in the 60s; who were they?

12 Which soccer manager took Coventry City into the First Division?

13 Of which 60s soccer team was Bill Shankly manager?

14 For which team did Joe Corrigan keep goal in the mid 60s?

15 For whom did future England boss Bobby Robson play (and then manage briefly)?

. . . .

ANSWERS

1. Tottenham Hotspur 2, Manchester United 3, Glasgow Celtic 4, Jock Stein 5, Inter Milan 6, 2-1 7, Gemmell and Chalmers 8, Manchester United 9, 1968 10, Matt Busby 11, Bobby and Jack Charlton 12, Jimmy Hill 13, Liverpool 14, Manchester City 15, Fulham

QUIZ 69
POT LUCK

. . . .

1 What post did Sir Edward Compton take in 1967?

2 Which new capital city was inaugurated in 1960?

3 Where were the first "open" tennis championships held in Britain?

4 Which lone sailor came home from a round-the-world voyage in April 1969?

5 Can you name his yacht?

6 What day was celebrated on 23 April throughout the 60s?

7 Which new coins first appeared in 1968?

8 Which Russian cosmonaut died in 1967 during re-entry?

9 Which US submarine stayed submerged for three months in 1960?

10 Which recently opened seaway could ships use in North America?

11 Which two territories combined to form Tanzania?

12 When did this union take place?

13 Under whose leadership?

14 Which exhibition ran from April to October 1967 in Canada?

15 Where?

. . . .

ANSWERS

1, Britain's first Ombudsman 2, Brasilia 3, Bournemouth 4, Robin Knox-Johnston 5, "Suhaili" 6, St George's Day! 7, 5p and 10p decimal coins 8, Vladimir Komarov 9, USS "Triton" 10, The St Lawrence Seaway (opened April 1959) 11, Tanganyika and Zanzibar 12, 1964 13, Julius Nyerere 14, Expo 67 15, In Montreal

ARTS & ENTERTAINMENT

- **1** Who was the star of the film Star! ?
- **2** On whose career was the film based?
- **3** In which city was the thriller Bullitt set?
- **4** Was *Bullitt* famous for its car chase, gun-fights, or lengthy card game?
- **5** Who directed the 1969 Western *The Wild Bunch*?
- **6** Who wrote the play *The Royal Hunt of the Sun*?
- **7** Was this play set in a) South America b) India or c) China?
- **8** Which comic actress played a lesbian in a 1969 film?
- **9** What was the film?
- **10** In which Oscar-winning film musical did Harry Secombe and Mark Lester appear?
- **11** Which part did Oliver Reed play in this film?
- **12** Harry Secombe also appeared in a musical based on a favourite Dickens character: as who?
- **13** Which actress starred in *The Prime of Miss Jean Brodie*?
- **14** Which country gave the world the movie *I Am Curious (Yellow)*?
- **15** Why was the film controversial?

ANSWERS

1, Julie Andrews 2, Gertrude Lawrence 3, San Francisco 4, Car chase 5, Sam Peckinpah 6, Peter Shaffer 7, a) South Africa 8, Beryl Reid 9, *The Killing of Sister George* 10, *Oliver!* 11, Bill Sikes 12, Mr Pickwick 13, Maggie Smith 14, Sweden 15, It was sexually explicit for the time

SCIENCE & TECHNOLOGY

. . . .

1 What device had Jack St Clair Kilby just developed as the 60s began?

2 Were there floppy discs in the 60s?

3 What new way of "writing" came along in 1963?

4 Could 60s computers write music?

5 What were the Unimates (1962)

6 What had horizontal drums for the first time in 1960?

7 Was Velcro a 60s invention?

8 Did people in the 60s have metal detectors?

9 Did people use post-it notes in 1965?

10 How did most early 60s office staff make copies of letters they wrote?

11 What was the newest piece of officer equipment in 1960?

12 What was the 1968 Hobie Cat?

13 Which company developed the first mini tape cassette?

14 What year?

15 How long was the tape?

. . . .

ANSWERS

1, The integrated circuit. 2, Yes (they were a 1950 invention) 3, The light pen 4, Yes (first done 1956) 5, The first industrial robots 6, Washing machines 7, No (1940s) 8, Yes (1930s idea) 9, No 10, They used carbon-paper in typewriters 11, The photocopier (from Xerox) 12, A very light sailing boat 13, Philips 14, 1963 15, 100 mm

QUIZ 72
PEOPLE

. . . .

1 For what was Susie Cooper famous?

2 What was the name of the poet-laureate's son, later to be a famous actor?

3 Government minister Duncan Sandys was divorced in 1960; who was his wife?

4 Which future Scottish international joined Celtic in 1967?

5 Which children's writer wrote the screenplay for a 1964 Bond movie?

6 What was the film?

7 Hugh Dalton died in 1962; what post-war post had he held?

8 Who was the author of *French Provincial Cooking* (1960)?

9 Who was the first Welshman to win an Olympic gold medal?

10 When and where?

11 In which event?

12 Which actor starred as the doctor in the 1965 film *Dr Who and the Daleks*?

13 With which company did he make a number of horror films?

14 Who wrote about lateral thinking in 1967?

15 Which Scottish politician won his first seat as an MP at Aberdeen in 1966?

. . . .

ANSWERS

QUIZ 73
ARTS & ENTERTAINMENT

1 Who directed the film *Midnight Cowboy*?

2 Who were the film's two stars?

3 Which of these two also starred in *The Graduate*?

4 Opera singer Belle Silverman was better known by her stage name of …?

5 Was Joan Baez a) a folk singer b) a ballet dancer or c) a film star?

6 What were the first names of the Smothers Brothers?

7 Who wrote *The Love Machine*?

8 Who wrote the play *Inadmissible Evidence*?

9 Which World War II air battle was commemorated by a blockbuster film in 1969?

10 Which actress danced on screen in *Isadora*?

11 Which variety theatre did British TV viewers visit on Sunday nights?

12 Biggles was a children's TV favourite; was he a footballer, a pilot, or a naughty schoolboy?

13 Who wrote the Biggles stories?

14 Which comedian starred in *Citizen James*?

15 In which TV series did Hoss and Little Joe appear?

ANSWERS

1, John Schlesinger 2, Jon Voight and Dustin Hoffman 3, Dustin Hoffman 4, Beverly Sills 5, a) A folk singer 6, Tommy and Dickie 7, Jacqueline Susann 8, John Osborne 9, The Battle of Britain 10, Vanessa Redgrave 11, The London Palladium 12, A pilot 13, Captain W E Johns 14, Sid James 15, Bonanza

POT LUCK

. . . .

1 Which new path for walkers opened in 1965 in Britain?

2 Whom did Jimmy Ellis beat to win the world heavyweight boxing title in 1968?

3 Why had Muhammad Ali had the title taken away in 1967?

4 The first woman to sit in the House of Commons died in 1964; who was she?

5 Who rode in "Freedom 7"?

6 Where did Princess Margaret get married in 1960?

7 What ran for the last time in London in 1962?

8 The star of *High Noon*, he died in 1961. Who was he?

9 To whom was a memorial opened at Runnymede in 1965?

10 Which group of workers were on strike in Britain in 1966, for the first time since 1911?

11 What year did a substitute first come on during an English FA Cup Final?

12 For which team?

13 Was this the first year substitutes had been allowed?

14 Sir Geoffrey de Havilland, who died in 1965, was a designer of … what?

15 In which country was there a 1964 soccer riot in which 301 people were killed?

. . . .

ANSWERS

1. The Pennine Way, 2. Jerry Quarry 3. Because he refused to serve in the US military 4. Nancy, Lady Astor 5. Alan Shepard, the first American in space 6. Westminster Abbey 7. Trolleybuses 8. Gary Cooper 9. President John Kennedy 10. Seamen 11. 1968 12. West Bromwich Albion 13. No, they were legal in 1967 but not used 14. Aircraft 15. Peru

QUIZ 75
ARTS & ENTERTAINMENT

. . . .

1 Which TV character was created by actor Patrick McGoohan?

2 Who played The Saint long before he was 007?

3 Which TV detective was played by actor Rupert Davies?

4 On whose detective novels were these TV shows based?

5 Were the stories set in a) London b) New York c) Paris?

6 Which show spawned the catch-phrase in song "Cookie, Cookie, lend me your comb?"

7 What was the name of the popular cops show set in and around Honolulu?

8 Who was the star of the series?

9 What kind of animal was TV's Hammy?

10 What kind of performers were the stars of *Four Feather Falls*?

11 Who was Harry in the comedy series *Here's Harry*?

12 Who played the hellfire preacher in *Elmer Gantry*?

13 Which composer was the subject of the 1960 biopic *Song Without End*?

14 In which 60s Disney film was John Mills marooned on an island with his family?

15 In which TV series did Bill Fraser and Alfie Bass star as ex-soldiers?

. . . .

ANSWERS

1, Danger Man 2, Roger Moore 3, Inspector Maigret 4, Georges Simenon's 5, c) Paris 6, 77 Sunset Strip 7, *Hawaii Five-O* 8, Jack Lord 9, A hamster 10, Puppets 11, Harry Worth 12, Burt Lancaster 13, Franz Liszt 14, *The Swiss Family Robinson* 15, Bootsie and Snudge

QUIZ 76
SPORT
THE 1966 WORLD CUP

· ·

1 Which country's goalkeeper appeared in a record fifth World Cup competition in 1966?

2 Who was England's goalkeeper in the 1966 World Cup Finals?

3 Who was the only Blackpool player in the England team?

4 Which star striker was left out of the England line-up for the final?

5 What was the score in England's first match, against Uruguay?

6 Who scored both goals in England's win over France?

7 Which Argentine player was sent off during the quarter-final match against England?

8 What was the score in this match?

9 Whom did England beat in the semi-final?

10 Who was regarded as Portugal's star player, with nine goals in the tournament?

11 Whom did England beat in the 1966 World Cup Final?

12 What was the score in the final?

13 Which England player scored three goals in the World Cup Final win?

14 Who scored the other England goal?

15 Who was captain of the West German team?

· ·

ANSWERS

15, Uwe Seeler
11, West Germany 12, 4-2 (after extra time) 13, Geoff Hurst 14, Martin Peters
5, 0-0 6, Roger Hunt 7, Rattin 8, 1-0 to England 9, Portugal, 2-1 10, Eusebio
1, Mexico's Antonio Carvajal 2, Gordon Banks 3, Alan Ball 4, Jimmy Greaves

QUIZ 77
ARTS & ENTERTAINMENT

. . . .

1 In which 1960 film did Kirk Douglas play a slave leader?

2 Which Hollywood star played alongside Kirk Douglas in this movie and also *The Vikings*?

3 Who was the famous wife of this star?

4 And in which 60s film did she take a shower with fatal consequences?

5 Directed by?

6 In which 1960 film did Jack Lemmon have a valuable door key?

7 Who supplied his romantic interest and happy ending in this film?

8 And who was her real-life actor-brother?

9 In which 1960 film did John Wayne play Davy Crockett?

10 For which 1960 film did Elizabeth Taylor win a best-actress Oscar?

11 Who presented the TV talent show *Opportunity Knocks*?

12 Which US embarassment-show was presented in the UK by Bob Monkhouse?

13 *United* was a 60s TV soap – about what?

14 What was the setting for another 60s soap, *Compact*?

15 Famous on radio for *Family Favourites* and on British TV for *Tonight*; who was he?

. . . .

ANSWERS

QUIZ 78
PEOPLE

. . . .

1 Which English cricketer was nicknamed "Lord Ted"

2 And who was "Fiery Fred"?

3 Who was known as the "Louisville Lip"?

4 Was Frank Dunlop a) a stage director b) a tyre maker or c) a racing driver?

5 Which poet worked as a librarian at Hull University?

6 Which was the Queen Mother's favourite Scottish home?

7 Which journalist became editor of *The Sunday Times* in 1967?

8 For which party did Winnie Ewing win a famous 1967 victory at the polls?

9 In which constituency?

10 Which footballer pursued a celebrated legal case for players' freedom of contract?

11 For which club was he then playing?

12 Which actor, later a star of *Yes, Minister,* made his stage debut in 1961?

13 Whom did Floyd Patterson beat to regain the world heavyweight boxing title in 1960?

14 What nationality was his opponent?

15 What did Giovanni Battista Montini become in 1963?

. . . .

ANSWERS

1. Ted Dexter, 2. Fred Trueman 3. Cassius Clay (Muhammad Ali) 4, a) A stage director 5. Philip Larkin 6. The Castle of Mey 7. Harold Evans 8. Scottish Nationalists 9. Hamilton 10. George Eastham 11. Newcastle United 12. Paul Eddington 13. Ingemar Johansson 14. Swedish 15. Pope Paul VI

SCIENCE & TECHNOLOGY

1 Telecoms satellites were new in the 60s, but which writer predicted them back in 1946?

2 What year was the first experimental telecoms satellite launched?

3 And when did a practical satellite system become effective?

4 What new TV data system was shown in 1963?

5 What was the Stretch of 1961?

6 Which basic unit did it pioneer?

7 And how many bits make a byte?

8 When did time-sharing on computers begin?

9 Did schoolchildren have calculators in 1960 ?

10 What were mainframes?

11 What is BASIC?

12 And what year did it appear?

13 Was it invented in a) the USA b) France c) Japan?

14 What does BASIC stand for?

15 Which computer language was named after a French mathematician?

ANSWERS

1. Arthur C Clarke 2. 1960 3. 1962 4. Teletext 5. An IBM computer 6. The byte 7. Eight 8. 1962 9. No 10. Large computers – the kind used in the 60s 11. A computer language 12. 1965 13. a) The USA 14. Beginners' All Purpose Symbolic Instruction Code 15. Pascal

QUIZ 80
ARTS & ENTERTAINMENT

. . . .

1 Which TV panellist, famous for his grumpiness, collapsed and died outside the BBC in 1960?

2 Who was the interviewer in the TV series *Face to Face*?

3 Which former Goon starred in a TV show called *It's A Square World*?

4 Mack Sennett, who died in 1960, was famous for which silent-film comic creation?

5 What was the name of Anthony Perkins' character in *Psycho*?

6 Did he run a) a motel b) a garage or c) a drive-in restaurant?

7 What happened to Marion Crane when she visited him?

8 John Gavin, who also starred in Psycho, later became: a) US Ambasador to Mexico b) head of 20th Century Fox or c) Prime Minister of Australia?

9 This blue-eyed actor became "Fast Eddie" in *The Hustler*: name?

10 Which 60s musical film starred Natalie Wood as Maria?

11 Hayley appeared in *Whistle Down The Wind*. Who was her famous father?

12 Which TV comedy show was set in the London fashion business?

13 Which actress starred in this show as a shop steward?

14 Which actress appeared in the TV science fiction thriller *A for Andromeda* as an android?

15 *Wonderland by Night* was a 1961 hit for which German bandleader?

. . . .

ANSWERS

1, Gilbert Harding 2, John Freeman 3, Michael Bentine 4, The Keystone Kops 5, Norman Bates 6, a) A motel 7, She was murdered (she was played by Janet Leigh) 8, a) US Ambassador to Mexico 9, Paul Newman 10, *West Side Story* 11, John Mills 12, *The Rag Trade* 13, Miriam Karlin 14, Julie Christie 15, Bert Kaempfert

QUIZ 81
PEOPLE

. . . .

1 For what was Lucian Freud famous ?

2 Who wrote a 1963 novel called *The Perfect Fool*?

3 From what artistic activity did Christopher Gable retire in 1967?

4 What is David Frost's middle name?

5 Who refused to accept his party's 1960 vote on disarmament?

6 Which fashion designer was born in Gibraltar in 1961?

7 What post did Lord Gardiner hold in 1964?

8 Which soccer star was born in Gateshead in 1967?

9 Who was Britain's First Secretary of State in 1964?

10 Who resigned from the government in July 1966, but was back in August?

11 Of what was Charles Gibbs a respected historian a) fishing b) aviation or c) cricket?

12 In which sport was Irishman Mike Gibson a star?

13 In which newspaper group's papers did Giles cartoons appear?

14 Which artists called themselves "singing sculptures"?

15 Their full names?

. . . .

ANSWERS

1, Painting 2, Roy Fuller 3, Ballet dancing 4, Paradine 5, Hugh Gaitskell 6, John Galliano 7, Lord Chancellor 8, Paul Gascoigne 9, George Brown 10, George Brown 11, b) Aviation 12, Rugby Union football 13, The Express 14 Gilbert and George 15, Gilbert Proesch and George Passmore

QUIZ 82
POT LUCK

1 Which show closed after a record-breaking run at London's Victoria Palace Theatre?

2 How long had Coventry's new cathedral taken to build?

3 Who was its architect?

4 Where was soccer's 1967 European Cup Final played?

5 Where did Sharks and Jets meet on screen?

6 What kind of shop did Brian Epstein run before he managed the Beatles?

7 In which book does Captain Yossarian appear?

8 What did British Guiana become in 1966?

9 Zola Budd, later a controversial athlete, was born in 1966 – in which country?

10 What was different about horse racing starts in Britain after 1965?

11 What did Fred Baldasare of the USA do in 1962?

12 Which two countries were linked by a new road tunnel in 1965?

13 Through which mountain was it dug?

14 Who drove a car very fast over Lake Eyre in 1964?

15 Where is it?

ANSWERS

15, Australia
14, Donald Campbell 13, Mont Blanc 12, France and Italy 11, He swam the Channel underwater 10, Starting stalls were introduced 9, South Africa 8, Guyana 7, *Catch 22* 6, A record shop 5, In the film of *West Side Story* 4, Lisbon 3, Sir Basil Spence 2, Six years 1, *The Black and White Minstrel Show*

QUIZ 83
SPORT

. . . .

1 Who captained England to their 1966 World Cup victory?

2 By what first name was US tennis star Charles McKinley usually called?

3 Whom did Terry Downes beat in April 1961 to win a world boxing title?

4 The "Georgia Peach" died in April 1961; who was this US baseball legend?

5 In April 1961 England's soccer team trounced Scotland at Wembley; what was the score?

6 In which sport did Notre Dame triumph in 1966?

7 Which famous soccer player refused to appear on the TV show *This Is Your Life*?

8 For which home country did he play international football?

9 Which English soccer team set a record by winning the first 10 games of the 1960–61 season?

10 Which American football team won the NFL title in 1961 and 1962?

11 Which team won the SuperBowl in 1966–67 and again in 1967–68?

12 How many times did Jack Nicklaus win the US Open in the 60s?

13 For which country did John Snow play cricket?

14 Which golfer won both the US Open and PGA titles in 1960?

15 What year did the USA and Great Britain tie the Ryder Cup?

. . . .

ANSWERS

1, Bobby Moore 2, Chuck 3, Paul Pender 4, Ty Cobb 5, 9-3 6, American college football 7, Danny Blanchflower 8, Northern Ireland 9, Tottenham Hotspur 10, Green Bay 11, Green Bay 12, Twice (1962 and 1967) 13, England 14, Arnold Palmer 15, 1969

QUIZ 84

MUSIC

1960

• •

1 Complete the 1960 chart-topping title: *Itsby Bitsy Teeny Weeny* …

2 Who took this to number one in Britain in August 1960?

3 Who had a British number 1 in 1960 with *What Do You Want to Make Those Eyes at Me For?*

4 Which US singer topped the charts with *El Paso*?

5 What was the title of Johnny Preston's "Native American" chart-topper?

6 Who led his orchestra to *A Summer Place*?

7 What was Lonnie Donegan's Ole Man?

8 Which patch-eyed band were shakin' all over in August 1960?

9 What did Jimmy Jones claim he had in his 1960 hit song?

10 Which Brenda was sorry in July 1960?

11 Which Everly Brothers' smash had a circus sound to it?

12 What did Ricky Valance urge record-buyers …?

13 Who sang *Save The Last Dance For Me*?

14 With which group were Hank Marvin and Bruce Welch enjoying the bright lights in 1960?

15 Which solo singer did they back?

• •

ANSWERS

15, Cliff Richard

11, *Cathy's Clown* 12, *Tell Laura I Love Her* 13, The Drifters 14, The Shadows

and the Pirates 9, *Good Timin'* 10, Brenda Lee, with her hit song *I'm Sorry*

4, Marty Robbins 5, *Running Bear* 6, Percy Faith 7, A Dustman 8, Johnny Kidd

1, *Yellow Polka Dot Bikini* 2, Brian Hyland 3, Emile Ford and the Checkmates

PEOPLE

. . . .

1 Percussionist, born Aberdeen in 1965; later became deaf. Name?

2 Who wrote *The Spire* (1964)?

3 Which cricketer caused a fuss by moving from Gloucestershire to Worcestershire?

4 Why did this move arouse comment?

5 Whose first play was *Wise Child* (1967)?

6 Whose Bazar store sold the first miniskirts?

7 What post did Denis Healey hold in 1964?

8 Who wrote *Eleven Poems* (1965)?

9 Which British big band leader died in 1969?

10 Who was the Catholic Archbishop of Westminster who died in 1963?

11 Which comic's real name was Alfred Hawthorne?

12 In which film did he play a toymaker?

13 The radio doctor got to lead the BBC in 1967; who was he?

14 Who wrote a biography of Lytton Strachey?

15 Who played Prince Hal and Richard II at Stratford in 1963–64?

. . . .

ANSWERS

1. Evelyn Glennie 2. William Golding 3. Tom Graveney 4. Transfers were then frowned upon in county cricket 5. Simon Gray 6. Mary Quant 7. Defence Secretary 8. Seamus Heaney 9. Ted Heath 10. Cardinal John Heenan 11. Benny Hill 12. *Chitty Chitty Bang Bang* 13. Charles Hill 14. Michael Holroyd 15. Ian Holm

QUIZ 86
MUSIC

• •

1 Who recorded *Spanish Harlem* in 1960?

2 With which separate hits did Elvis Presley chart-top both sides of the Atlantic in December 1960?

3 Which record was the first to be played on BBC's new Radio One in 1967?

4 Whose 60s hits included *Poor Me*?

5 Which 60s group had a drummer named Keith Moon?

6 Which group recorded the 1965 hit *The Carnival is Over*?

7 Complete the 60s group name. Freddy and the …?

8 Strawberry Alarm Clock topped the US charts in 1967 with *Incense and Peppermints*. True or false?

9 Which veteran jazz musician topped the charts in 1968 with *What A Wonderful World*?

10 Who spotted singer Mary Hopkin on a British TV show and recommended her to Paul McCartney: a) Twiggy b) Bob Dylan c) Janis Joplin?

11 What was the name of the Beatles' own record label?

12 Whose *Ode to Billy Joe* was a 1967 hit?

13 The Beatles' manager died in 1967. What was his name?

14 *Waterloo Sunset* was a 1967 hit … for which British group?

15 Which 60s singer's real name was Ronald Wycherley?

• •

ANSWERS

1, Ben E King 2, *It's Now or Never* (UK), *Are You Lonesome Tonight* (USA) 3, *Flowers in the Rain* by The Move 4, Adam Faith 5, The Who 6, The Seekers 7, Dreamers 8, True 9, Louis Armstrong 10, a) Twiggy 11, Apple 12, Bobby Gentry 13, Brian Epstein 14, The Kinks 15, Billy Fury

QUIZ 87
SCIENCE & TECHNOLOGY

. . . .

1 In 1960, how old was the microchip?

2 Who were the "Fairchildren"?

3 Where was print first typeset by computer?

4 What year?

5 What was PROLOG?

6 What was diazepan?

7 By what other name did it become well known?

8 Which Arabian antelope was feared to be endangered by hunting?

9 Which large sea mammals were the focus of anti-hunting campaigns?

10 Which Californian bird was rescued from the brink of extinction?

11 Which was Madagascar's rarest lemur?

12 Which Mediterranean seal was hit by pollution and habitat loss?

13 Which "extinct" Tasmanian marsupial continued to excite reports of its survival?

14 Which animal became the symbol of the World Wildlife Fund?

15 Which chemical was blamed for the decline in numbers of birds of prey ?

. . . .

ANSWERS

1, About a year 2, A group of US computer engineers who left Fairchild and set up on their own 3, West Germany 4, 1965 5, A computer language 6, A tranquilliser 7, Valium 8, The oryx 9, Whales 10, The Californian condor 11, The aye-aye 12, The monk seal 13, The thylacine 14, The giant panda 15, DDT

QUIZ 88
PEOPLE

. . . .

1. Was Dame Barbara Hepworth a painter, dancer or sculptor?
2. In which sport was Reg Harris famous?
3. Which actress starred in the 1969 play *Plaza Suite*?
4. Who wrote the play?
5. Who was Britain's Minister of Overseas Development in 1969?
6. Which actor's real name was Hirsch Larushka Skikne?
7. In which film did he play a brainwashed soldier?
8. Which rugby star was born in Edinburgh in 1962?
9. Which climber scaled the north face of the Matterhorn in 1967?
10. Who became Labour MP for Birmingham Sparkbrook in 1964?
11. Which young and brilliant scientist contracted a disabling neuromotor disease?
12. Who became director of the Covent Garden Opera in 1969?
13. Was Richard Hamilton a painter, poet or cricketer?
14. Which cartoon character had Frank Hampson famously illustrated?
15. In which children's comic?

. . . .

ANSWERS

MUSIC

. . . .

1 Which singer was called a "Judas" for switching from acoustic to electric guitar in concert in 1966?

2 Which concept album from the Beatles excited the critics in 1967?

3 Who had a hit with *A Whiter Shade of Pale* in 1967?

4 Which dance did Chubby Checker sing about in 1961?

5 In 1962 Robert Zimmerman signed for CBS records; by what name did he become a star?

6 Which American dj was tried on charges of "payola" in 1962?

7 Was the Tornadoes' 1962 hit *Telstar* a vocal or instrumental?

8 *Big Girls Don't Cry* and *Sherry* were two hits by this 60s group. Name?

9 What year did the Rolling Stones have their first UK number one?

10 Rick Savage, drummer, was born in December 1960. With which rock band did he achieve success?

11 Which Beatle was deported from Germany in December 1960 for being an under-age worker?

12 Who had a hit with *Only the Lonely* in 1960?

13 Which Indian tribe was the title of a 1960 Shadows hit?

14 *Will You Love Me Tomorrow?* was a big US hit in 1960 for which group?

15 Who sang *Move Over Darling*?

. . . .

ANSWERS

1, Bob Dylan 2, The *Sergeant Pepper* album 3, Procol Harum 4, The Twist 5, Bob Dylan 6, Alan Freed 7, Instrumental 8, The Four Seasons 9, 1964 10, Def Leppard 11, George Harrison 12, Roy Orbison 13, *Apache* 14, The Shirelles 15, Doris Day

QUIZ 90
PEOPLE

. . . .

1 Which comic transferred his half hour from radio to TV in 1962?

2 In which film did he appear in 1963?

3 For which crime was James Hanratty hanged in 1962?

4 From which magazine did Bert Hardy retire in 1967?

5 For what was he best known?

6 Which event did Lord Harewood direct from 1960 to 65?

7 Which former England batsman and cricket captain died in 1965?

8 Which was Jimmy Greaves' first League soccer club?

9 Who wrote *A Burnt Out Case* (1961)?

10 In 1969 the same author wrote *Travels With …*?

11 Who was his brother, who became Director General of the BBC?

12 At which university was Germaine Greer lecturing in 1968?

13 Which British dancer appeared with the Chinese Ballet in 1964?

14 Which poet wrote *My Sad Captains* (1961)?

15 Which star athlete was born in Chigwell in 1966?

. . . .

ANSWERS

1, Tony Hancock 2, *The Punch and Judy Man* 3, The A6 murder of 1961 4, *Picture Post* 5, Photographs 6, The Edinburgh Festival 7, Walter Hammond 8, Chelsea 9, Graham Greene 10, *My Aunt* 11, Hugh Carleton Greene 12, Warwick 13, Beryl Grey 14, Thom Gunn 15, Sally Gunnell

QUIZ 91
WORLD EVENTS
1961

. . . .

1 Which accused person refused to swear on a Bible?

2 Where did President Po Sun Yun resign?

3 Who was told he was "a missile guided at the hearts of the British people"?

4 What did he do on 14 July?

5 Where was Rudolf Nureyev when he defected to the West?

6 How long did Virgil Grissom fly in space in July?

7 Why was General Salan sentenced to death?

8 Which country's population now topped 52 million?

9 Which famous writer died at home in Idaho, probably by his own hand?

10 Why was Canon Collins arrested in London?

11 Which London square was the focus for CND protests?

12 Who was nicknamed Old Goatbeard by West Berliners?

13 What were found at Fishbourne in Sussex?

14 What did Britain apply to join in August 1961?

15 Where did Nkrumah sack his army commander?

. . . .

ANSWERS

1, Adolf Eichmann 2, South Korea 3, Yuri Gagarin 4, Visited Britain 5 Le Bourget airport, France 6, 16 minutes 7, For his part in the failed coup in French Algeria 8, Britain's 9, Ernest Hemingway 10, There were disturbances during a ban-the-bomb rally 11, Trafalgar Square 12, Walter Ulbricht, leader of East Germany 13, Roman mosaics, part of a huge Romano-British palace 14, The EEC 15, Ghana

QUIZ 92
POT LUCK

- -

1 What did Nan Winton do for the first time on British TV in 1960?

2 How was "Britannia" propelled across the Atlantic in 1969?

3 What ran between Wallasey and Rhyl for the first time in 1962?

4 Which screen actor famous for his role as Sherlock Holmes died in 1967?

5 Which river was spanned by the Runcorn Bridge in 1961?

6 From whom did the Maldive Islands gain independence in 1965?

7 In which ocean are they?

8 Who made his last appearance in the House of Commons in 1964?

9 What happened to Britain's steel industry in 1967?

10 What first did Michael Darbellay of Switzerland achieve in 1963?

11 Which judicially significant events took place at Walton and Strangeways gaols in 1964?

12 Why did Swedish drivers have to take extra care after 2 September 1967?

13 How old was Ho Chi Minh of North Vietnam when he died in 1969?

14 Which famous medical missionary died at Lambarene in West Africa in 1965?

15 Which listings magazine went on sale from September 1968?

- -

ANSWERS

1, Read the news 2, By oars 3, A hovercraft service 4, Basil Rathbone 5, The Mersey 6, Britain 7, Indian Ocean 8, Sir Winston Churchill 9, It was renationalized 10, First solo ascent of the north wall of the Eiger 11, Britain's last hangings 12, They switched to driving on the right side of the road 13, 79 14, Albert Schweitzer 15, *TV Times*

QUIZ 93
PEOPLE

. . . .

1 For what were Halas and Batchelor famous?

2 Writer on science, Marxist, died 1964; who was he?

3 Whose 1960 life story was entitled *Sing As We Go*?

4 What did Fred Hoyle teach at Cambridge?

5 Who became player-manager of Leeds United in 1961?

6 Who showed her first dresses in 1969?

7 Who wrote *The Wide Sargasso Sea* (1966)?

8 What nationality was artist Ceri Richards?

9 Which former actress was married to John Profumo?

10 Whose first film as producer was called *S.W.A.L.K*?

11 After whom was Rachmanism named?

12 And what was it?

13 Author of *Swallows and Amazons*, he died in1962. Name?

14 Who wrote a play called *Ross*?

15 And who was its subject?

. . . .

ANSWERS

QUIZ 94
SPORT

· ·

1 In which sport was Mihkail Voronin a Sixties star?

2 Which racehorse won the 1964 Kentucky Derby?

3 In 1961 the Chicago Black Hawks won … what?

4 For which country did Bobby Simpson play cricket?

5 Giacomo Agostini was world champion … in what?

6 Which country won seven Davis Cups in the 1960s?

7 Did Britain win the Wightman Cup during the 60s?

8 By what name were Toronto's all-conquering 60s ice hockey team known?

9 Ford and Towler were British world champions … in what?

10 In which sport did Mike Hailwood win a world title in 1962?

11 Which festive horse won the 1964 English Derby?

12 Who was the jockey?

13 In what event was Willie Davenport a track star?

14 In which track event did Ann Packer of Britain win Olympic gold in 1964?

15 In which event did she win silver?

· ·

ANSWERS

1, Gymnastics 2, Northern Dancer 3, The Stanley Cup, for ice hockey 4, Australia 5, Motor cycling 6, Australia 7, Yes (1960 and 1968) 8, Maple Leafs 9, Ice dancing 10, Motor cycling 11, Santa Claus 12, Scobie Breasley 13, Hurdles (110 metres) 14, 800 metres 15, The 400 metres

QUIZ 95
PEOPLE

. . . .

1 Who joined *Braden's Week* as a reporter in 1968?

2 Who became editor of *The Times* in 1967?

3 Which writer created Chief Inspector Wexford?

4 What year was her first novel published?

5 *A Cab At The Door* was the 1968 autobiography of … who?

6 What was actor Michael Hordern's other great love?

7 About what did Sir Brian Horrocks talk on TV?

8 Which actor made his stage debut in *Romeo and Juliet*, at Stoke on Trent in 1969?

9 Which comedian starred in *A Funny Thing Happened On The Way To The Forum*?

10 Who was Bishop of Stepney?

11 Who wrote a play called *The Reluctant Peer* (1963)?

12 Why was it appropriate?

13 The author of *Brave New World* died in 1963; who was he?

14 Who captained the England cricket team to victory against West Indies in 1969?

15 Who founded the magazine *Private Eye*?

. . . .

ANSWERS

1, Esther Rantzen 2, William Rees-Mogg 3, Ruth Rendell 4, 1964 5, V S Pritchett 6, Fishing 7, Military history 8, Bob Hoskins 9, Frankie Howerd 10, Trevor Huddlestone 11, William Douglas Home 12, He was the brother of Lord Home, prime minister 13, Aldous Huxley 14, Ray Illingworth 15, Richard Ingrams

MUSIC

. . . .

1 Which US singer had *Georgia on My Mind*?

2 At which club did the Beatles make their first appearance in March 1961?

3 Which singer had a 1961 hit with *Runaway*?

4 Whose recording of *I Wanna Be Your Man* set them on the road to success in 1964?

5 Who wrote *I Wanna Be Your Man*?

6 Why were the Beatles at Buckingham Palace in 1965?

7 In 1961 Frank Sinatra formed his own record label. Its name?

8 Who were Gladys Knight's backing group?

9 Which rock singer died in the 1960 car crash that left Gene Vincent injured?

10 Which girl singer recorded *You Don't Know* in 1961?

11 Their first single was a song called *Buttered Popcorn* released by Motown in 1961. Who were they?

12 Eden Kane had a UK hit in 1961. Its title?

13 Hit albums in the 1960s and a popular TV show, but later branded racist for "blacking up". Who were they?

14 Which group first had a hit with *Please Mr Postman* (1961)?

15 Who was Bobby Vee asking listeners to *Take Good Care of …* in 1961?

. . . .

ANSWERS

1, Ray Charles 2, The Cavern, Liverpool 3, Del Shannon 4, The Rolling Stones 5, Lennon and McCartney 6, To receive their MBE awards 7, Reprise 8, The Pips 9, Eddie Cochran 10, Helen Shapiro 11, The Supremes 12, Well I Ask You 13, The Black and White Minstrels 14, The Marvelettes 15, My Baby

WORLD EVENTS
1961

. . . .

1 Which trades union was expelled from the British TUC for vote-rigging?

2 What nationality was the new UN secretary general?

3 Who was he?

4 Whom did he succeed?

5 Which central Asian state joined the UN?

6 Whose body was no longer to be seen in the Lenin Mausoleum in Moscow?

7 Which African state did the Queen visit in December?

8 Which province attempted to secede from the Congo?

9 Who was its leader?

10 Which Portuguese enclave was retaken by India?

11 Which European country had ruled it for 400 years?

12 By whom was US soldier James Davis killed?

13 Whom did plotters in France try to blow up in his car?

14 Which city was renamed Volgograd?

15 Who won a fourth term as his country's Chancellor?

. . . .

ANSWERS

1, The Electrical Trades Union 2, Burmese 3, U Thant 4, Dag Hammarskjold 5, Mongolia 6, Stalin's 7, Ghana 8, Katanga 9, Moise Tshombe 10, Goa 11, Portugal 12, The Vietcong (said to be the first US soldier so to die) 13, President De Gaulle 14, Stalingrad 15, Konrad Adenauer of West Germany

QUIZ 98
ARTS &
ENTERTAINMENT

· ·

1 The *Lion Sleeps Tonight* was a 1961 hit based on which African song?

2 What name did Carl and the Passions adopt in 1961?

3 Jacqueline Du Pré won acclaim as a musician, playing which instrument?

4 On what instrument did the flamboyant Liberace entertain his fans?

5 Which Dinah died in 1963 after a career as a jazz and blues singer?

6 The Weavers disbanded in 1963. Were they a) a folk group b) a string quartet c) a trad jazz band?

7 Which duo recorded *Hey Paula* in 1963?

8 Cliff Richard and the Shadows made a 1963 film about a post-spring vacation. What was its title?

9 How many US Top Ten hits did Cliff Richard have in the 60s: a) seven b) four c) none?

10 Which instruments did a) Ginger Baker and b) Eric Clapton play?

11 Which British group went to the top of the 1963 charts with *How Do You Do It?*

12 In which country was Johnny Halliday a pop star?

13 Complete this 60s American group's name: Johnny and the …?

14 Who backed Martha on the 1963 hit *Heatwave*?

15 With which of these groups did Jimmy Page make his name: a) Rolling Stones b) Dave Clark Five c) Yardbirds?

· ·

ANSWERS

1, *Wimoweh* 2, The Beach Boys 3, Cello 4, Piano 5, Dinah Washington 6, a) A folk group 7, Paul and Paula 8, *Summer Holiday* 9, c) None 10, a) Drums b) Guitar 11, Gerry and the Pacemakers 12, France 13, Hurricanes 14, The Vandellas 15, c) Yardbirds

PEOPLE

. . . .

1 Who designed the Mini car?

2 Who was the first Briton to win on the US golf tour, in 1968?

3 Which economist wrote *Spaceship Earth* in 1966?

4 Which Ulster politician founded the SDLP?

5 Who starred in *At The Drop Of Another Hat* (1963)?

6 To whom was Roberto Arias married?

7 Whose three brothers were Dingle, Hugh and John?

8 Which Welsh constituency did he represent from 1960?

9 Who compered *Sunday Night at the London Palladium* 1958-60?

10 Who wrote *The Collector* (1963)?

11 About which sport did C L R James write?

12 Where was he born?

13 Which union did Jack Jones lead?

14 Which actress starred in the film of *The French Lieutenant's Woman*?

15 Which poet stood for Parliament as a communist in 1963?

. . . .

ANSWERS

1, Alec Issigonis 2, Tony Jacklin 3, Barbara Jackson 4, Gerry Fitt 5, Flanders and Swan 6, Margot Fonteyn 7, Michael Foot 8, Ebbw Vale 9, Bruce Forsyth 10, John Fowles 11, Cricket 12, Trinidad 13, Transport and General (TGWU) 14, Meryl Streep 15, Hugh MacDiarmid

QUIZ 100
SPORT

. . . .

1 Which country did Betty Cuthbert represent?

2 And in which sport?

3 Randy Matson was a US athlete who … a)jumped b) threw or c) ran?

4 In which athletics event did Valery Brumel set new heights?

5 In which event was American Bill Toomey an all-round star?

6 In which sport was Australia's Dawn Fraser a star?

7 Michel Jazy was a 60s track star; what nationality was he?

8 Which Kenyan runner set a world record for 5000 metres in 1965?

9 With which sport do you associate Doug Walters?

10 And for which country did he play?

11 Clive Lloyd was a rising star, in which sport?

12 And for which national team?

13 John Edrich was a stalwart of which national cricket team?

14 How many runs did he score in an innings against New Zealand in 1965?

15 For which country did Bill Lawry play cricket?

. . . .

ANSWERS

1, Australia 2, Athletics 3, b) Threw, or rather he put the shot 4, High jump 5, Decathlon 6, Swimming 7, French 8, Kip Keino 9, Cricket 10, Australia 11, Cricket 12, West Indies 13, England 14, 310 (not out) 15, Australia

QUIZ 101
POT LUCK

. . . .

1 Where was the liner "QE2" launched?

2 Which student quiz show began in September 1962 on British TV?

3 Who was the presenter?

4 Which oil company found oil beneath the North Sea in 1965?

5 Which liner returned to Southampton for the last time in 1967?

6 Which country launched a satellite called *Alouette*?

7 What was Botswana called before independence in 1966?

8 What year did Nigeria become a republic?

9 Who was left on his own in Spandau prison after October 1966?

10 Who was the first pope to visit New York?

11 When?

12 What was Lesotho called before it became independent in 1966?

13 When were majority verdicts first given in British jury trials?

14 Where was Che Guevara killed?

15 What year?

. . . .

ANSWERS

QUIZ 102
PEOPLE

. . . .

1 Which future Scottish international soccer striker and TV celebrity was born in 1962?

2 Who was the "voice of tennis" during Wimbledon fortnight in Britain?

3 Which colourful comedian died in 1963?

4 Who was the co-author of *The Bed Sitting-Room*?

5 Who ran London's Mermaid Theatre?

6 Who was born Georgious Panayiotou in 1963?

7 *The American Way of Death* was written by …?

8 Who had a TV series called *Let Me Speak*?

9 Of which British university was he rector until he resigned in 1968?

10 Why did he resign?

11 Who started up her own fashion company in 1966?

12 Who was the founder of the Early Music Consort of London?

13 Who wore the bow tie on TV's *Call My Bluff*?

14 Who was his opposing team captain?

15 Who married Laurence Olivier in 1961?

. . . .

ANSWERS

1. Ally McCoist 2. Dan Maskell 3. Max Miller 4. Spike Milligan 5. Bernard Miles 6. George Michael 7. Jessica Mitford 8. Malcolm Muggeridge 9. Edinburgh 10. He said students were too liberal and promiscuous 11. Jean Muir 12. David Munrow 13. Frank Muir 14. Arthur Marshall 15. Joan Plowright

MUSIC

ELVIS

. . . .

1 Where was Elvis Presley born?

2 And the year?

3 In 1960 why had Elvis Presley been away from the studio for two years?

4 Was *It's Now or Never* a number one both sides of the Atlantic?

5 Which was Elvis' first 60s hit in Britain?

6 And what was his last number one in the decade?

7 What was unusual about Elvis Presley's seventh film *Wild In The Country*?

8 Presley's next film had a Pacific feel and a raft of hit songs; its name?

9 Whom did Elvis marry in 1967?

10 In which US city did Presley return to live appearances in the late 1960s?

11 Complete these Presley titles, both 60s hits; *Return to* ...

12 *Clean Up Your Own* ...

13 Which of these was not the title of a 60s Presley album: *Clambake, Speedway, Burger King*?

14 Which 60s Presley hit had a South American flavour?

15 Which Presley song included some German?

. . . .

ANSWERS

1, Tupelo, Mississippi 2, 1935 3, He had been in the US Army 4, Yes 5, Stuck on You 6, *Crying in the Chapel* (May 1965) 7, It originally had no songs (three were restored to soothe indignant fans) 8, Blue Hawaii 9, Priscilla Beaulieu 10, Las Vegas 11, *Sender* 12, *Back Yard* 13, *Burger King* 14, *Bossa Nova Baby* 15, *Wooden Heart*

QUIZ 104
WORLD EVENTS
1962

. . . .

1 In which country was the OAS a terrorist body?

2 Whom did the Pope excommunicate?

3 Which countries disagreed over a nuclear test ban?

4 Where were test ban talks held?

5 Which "forgotten" disease reappeared in Britain at Bradford?

6 Which British newspaper issued a colour supplement?

7 In which German city did flooding cause many deaths?

8 Which Kent suburb provided a by-election upset in Britain?

9 Who won?

10 Who was the victorious Liberal?

11 Who declared "Conservatism is young, virulent and alive …?

12 Who led the Congress Party to election success in India?

13 In which country did premier Michel Debré resign?

14 Which artist was awarded the Lenin Peace Prize?

15 With whom did he share it?

. . . .

ANSWERS

1, France 2, Fidel Castro 3, The USA and the USSR 4, Geneva 5, Smallpox 6, The Sunday Times 7, Hamburg 8, Orpington 9, The Liberals beat the Tories 10, Eric Lubbock 11, Senator Barry Goldwater 12, Nehru 13, France 14, Picasso 15, Kwame Nkrumah

QUIZ 105
MUSIC
1961

• •

1 *Poetry in Motion* was a 1961 hit for which US singer?

2 *Quarter to Three* was a 1961 hit … for who?

3 Which eccentric band crooned *You're Driving Me Crazy* in May 1961?

4 George O'Dowd was born in June 1961: under what name did he become an 80s pop star?

5 Who topped the US charts in 1961 with Tossin' And Turnin'?

6 With which song did The Highwaymen reach the charts in 1961?

7 What did the Everly Brothers set off to join in November 1961?

8 Which British singer recorded *Tower Of Strength*?

9 Who sang *Moon River* and ended 1961 with a British number one?

10 Which Liverpool group, whose members included Tony Crane and Billy Kinsley, formed in 1961?

11 Who was reaching for the stars and climbing every mountain in 1961?

12 Which actor-singer had a hit with *Johnny Remember Me*?

13 A Shadows hit had the same name as a raft that made an epic voyage; its title?

14 Ray Charles sang *Hit The Road* … who?

15 Dion's 1961 hit was about a flighty girl called Runaround … who?

• •

ANSWERS

1, Johnny Tillotson 2, Gary US Bonds 3, The Temperance Seven 4, Boy George 5, Bobby Lewis 6, Michael 7, The US Marines 8, Frankie Vaughan 9, Danny Williams 10, The Merseybeats 11, Shirley Bassey (who topped the UK charts with *Reach For The Stars/Climb Ev'ry Mountain*) 12, John Leyton 13, Kon-Tiki 14, Jack 15, Sue

QUIZ 106
PEOPLE

. . . .

1 With what kinds of books was C T Onions (died 1965) associated?

2 Who wrote the play *What The Butler Saw*?

3 How did this dramatist die in 1967?

4 Which fashion designer was brought up in Barnardo homes during the 60s?

5 Which future Rugby League star was born in London in 1966?

6 Whose fashion store chain was founded in 1968?

7 Which playwright wrote *Ironhand* (1963)?

8 Who built Occidental Petroleum into a giant?

9 Which black comedian was prominent in the US Civil Rights movement?

10 On which sport did Ron Pickering talk and coach?

11 Which historian was associated with *The Buildings of England* series?

12 Which saxophonist was born in London in 1964?

13 Which pop group was co-founded by Syd Barrett in 1965–66?

14 In which industry was Jimmy Knapp working?

15 Of what was Dame Kathleen Lonsdale a professor?

. . . .

ANSWERS

1, English dictionaries 2, Joe Orton 3, He was murdered 4, Bruce Oldfield 5, Martin Offiah 6, Laura Ashley's 7, John Arden 8, Armand Hammer 9, Dick Gregory 10, Athletics 11, Sir Nikolaus Pevsner 12, Courtney Pine 13, Pink Floyd 14, Railways 15, Chemistry

QUIZ 107
SPORT

. . . .

1 In which sport did Bob Seagren reach new heights?

2 What year did George Best make his debut for Manchester United?

3 How did boxer Rocky Marciano die in 1969?

4 In what sport was Tom Seaver a US star of 1967?

5 In what sport was Alan Rudkin a champion?

6 Maureen Connolly died in 1969; in which sport was she famous?

7 And what was her nickname?

8 What nationality was Jean-Claude Killy?

9 And what was his sport?

10 Which US athlete was described as a "one man track team"?

11 At which Olympics did he win a gold medal?

12 Which boxing title did Jack Bodell hold in 1969?

13 Tich Freeman died in 1965; in which sport had he been a record-breaker?

14 What was soccer player Keith Peacock's claim to fame in 1965?

15 For whom was he playing?

. . . .

ANSWERS

1, Pole vaulting 2, 1963 3, Plane crash 4, Baseball 5, Boxing 6, Tennis 7, Little Mo 8, French 9, Skiing 10, Rafer Johnson 11, Rome 1960 12, British heavyweight championship 13, Cricket 14, He was the first substitute used in a Football League soccer match 15, Charlton Athletic

PEOPLE

. . . .

1 Which writer, who died in 1962, was married to US poet Hilda Doolittle?

2 Who wrote *The Saliva Tree* (1966)?

3 Which thriller writer created a detective called Albert Campion?

4 Which TV naturalist became controller of BBC-2?

5 What nationality was biochemist Max Perutz?

6 What year did he win a Nobel Prize?

7 Who wrote a book called *My Silent War*?

8 Who was he?

9 Which pop group recorded the *Piper At The Gates of Dawn* album?

10 What did Dame Kathleen Kenyon investigate?

11 Who was chairman of International Publishing Corporation 1963–68?

12 For what did R B Kitaj make his name?

13 What year did Tim Rice and Andrew Loyd Webber meet?

14 What did Ewan MacColl do?

15 What did Hamish McInnes do?

. . . .

ANSWERS

1, Richard Aldington 2, Brian Aldiss 3, Margery Allingham 4, David Attenborough 5, Australian 6, 1962 7, Kim Philby 8, A spy 9, Pink Floyd 10, Biblical sites (she was an archaeologist) 11, Cecil King 12, As an artist 13, 1965 14, He was a folk singer 15, He climbed mountains

QUIZ 109
POT LUCK

. . . .

1 Which one of the Marx brothers played the piano?

2 What nationality was Edith Piaf?

3 What did she regret, according to her most famous song?

4 Which London railway station reopened in 1968 minus its famous arch?

5 What year did Cole Porter die?

6 What kind of business was founded by Elizabeth Arden?

7 Which member of the Crazy Gang died in October 1968?

8 To which TV series did this comedian provide the opening song?

9 Who was his stage partner?

10 Which future England soccer coach won his first cap as a player in 1964?

11 In which disaster did 116 children die, out of a total of 144 people killed?

12 Where was this tragedy?

13 And how did it happen?

14 In which US city was the Gateway to the West arch completed in 1965?

15 With which London theatre was John Dexter associated?

. . . .

ANSWERS

1. Chico (who died in 1961) 2. French 3. Nothing 4. Euston 5. 1964 6. Cosmetics 7. Bud Flanagan 8. *Dad's Army* 9. Chesney Allen 10. Terry Venables 11. The Aberfan disaster 12. South Wales, in mid Glamorgan 13. A coal tip slid down onto a village school 14. St Louis, Missouri 15. The Royal Court

ARTS & ENTERTAINMENT

1 Who took *Blue Moon* to the top of the US charts in 1961?

2 *On The Rebound* was a 1961 hit for which artiste?

3 Who played Rita Tushingham's mother in the film *A Taste of Honey*?

4 Complete the 1961 war film title, *The Guns of* …

5 What event was the subject of the film *Judgement at Nuremberg*?

6 Who starred in *Breakfast at Tiffany's*?

7 Which Saturday radio programme did Eamonn Andrews present?

8 Why were children disappointed by BBC radio planners in 1961?

9 Who first presented the BBC letters show *Points of View*?

10 In *The Seven Faces of Jim* comedy series, who was Jim?

11 Which well-proportioned comedienne partnered both Tony Hancock and Eric Sykes on radio and television?

12 She starred as Eth in radio's *Take It From Here* and was still *Absolutely Fabulous* in the 90s; who is she?

13 Which ukulele-strumming comedian left the stage in 1961?

14 An orchestral conductor famous for his barbed remarks and wit died in 1961; who was he?

15 Which band recorded an album called *Pet Sounds* in 1965?

ANSWERS

1. The Marcels 2. Floyd Cramer 3. Dora Bryan 4. *Navarone* 5. The Nazi war crimes trials after World War II 6. Audrey Hepburn 7. *Sports Report* 8. *Children's Hour* was scrapped 9. Robert Robinson 10. Jimmy Edwards 11. Hattie Jacques 12. June Whitfield 13. George Formby 14. Sir Thomas Beecham 15. The Beach Boys

QUIZ 111
PEOPLE

. . . .

1 Which theatrical knight-to-be made his stage debut at Coventry in 1961?

2 What was the Coventry theatre's name?

3 On which sport did Bill McLaren commentate (and still does)?

4 With which TV game show was Stuart Hall associated?

5 On which sport did Eddie Waring commentate?

6 Former player Jack Kramer became a TV pundit on which sport?

7 Whose wife married Kim Philby in 1966?

8 Where was Philby living?

9 What had her first husband been?

10 Who had been his accomplices?

11 Who wrote *When Eight Bells Toll*?

12 With which industry was Walter Marshall connected?

13 Who designed reclining figures for New York's Lincoln Center?

14 Which ex-soldier wrote *The Path to Leadership* (1961)?

15 Who retired as Chief of the Defence Staff in 1965?

. . . .

ANSWERS

Mountbatten
1, Ian McKellen 2, The Belgrade 3, Rugby union 4, It's A Knockout and later Jeux Sans Frontières 5, Rugby League 6, Tennis 7, Donald Maclean's 8, The USSR 9, A Soviet spy in British intelligence 10, Burgess, Philby and Blunt 11, Alastair Maclean 12, Nuclear research 13, Henry Moore 14, Montgomery 15, Lord

QUIZ 112
WORLD EVENTS

. . . .

1 In which country were taxes on washing machines and refrigerators cut?

2 Who said he was puzzled after hearing Benny Goodman play?

3 What were the new pandas on Britain's streets?

4 Who said hello to his new headmaster in Scotland?

5 To which Southeast Asian country did US Marines go in May 1962?

6 What did the initials SEATO stand for?

7 Which prime minister pruned his government in the "night of the long knives"?

8 Which French singer crooned to US viewers via satellite?

9 Who was punched on the jaw at a Union Movement meeting in London?

10 Which two Caribbean islands togther formed a new Commonwealth nation?

11 Who agreed to let Indonesia have western New Guinea?

12 Who was George Rockwell?

13 Who escaped a fourth assassination attempt in a year in France?

14 What did Commonwealth leaders tell Britain not to do?

15 Where did British troops fire tear gas at rioters in 1962?

. . . .

ANSWERS

1. Britain 2. Nikita Khrushchev 3. Pedestrian crossings 4. Prince Charles 5. Laos 6. South East Asia Treaty Organization 7. Harold Macmillan 8. Yves Montand 9. Sir Oswald Mosley 10. Trinidad and Tobago 11. The Netherlands 12. He led the American Nazis 13. General De Gaulle 14. Join the EEC 15. Aden

QUIZ 113
POT LUCK

- **1** What did RSG mean for British teenager TV viewers ?
- **2** Who was the show's girl presenter?
- **3** Who was "the Shrimp"?
- **4** Who starred in *The Cincinnatti Kid*?
- **5** Which Russian writer, author of *Quiet Flows the Don* won a Nobel prize in 1965?
- **6** Which animal escaped for the second time from London Zoo in December 1965?
- **7** What was stolen and later found in a garden by a dog named Pickles?
- **8** Where was Chi-Chi bound in the spring of 1966?
- **9** What was the object of this meeting?
- **10** Of what did Leslie O'Brien become governor in 1966?
- **11** What was different about the opening of Parliament in 1966?
- **12** What were Hoverlloyd offering passengers in 1966?
- **13** What was the BAA , set up in April 1966?
- **14** Whom did Sophia Loren marry in 1966?
- **15** Why did the Catholic Church disapprove?

ANSWERS

1, *Ready Steady Go* 2, Cathy McGowan 3, Model Jean Shrimpton 4, Steve McQueen 5, Mikhail Sholokhov 6, Goldie the eagle 7, The World Cup 8, To meet An-An, a male giant panda 9, To produce a giant panda cub in captivity (it did not succeed) 10, The Bank of England 11, It was televised for the first time 12, The first cross-channel hovercraft services 13, The British Airports Authority 14, Carlo Ponti 15, The groom was still married in the Church's eyes

QUIZ 114
ARTS & ENTERTAINMENT

1 Who hit the charts with *Walk Right Back* in 1961?

2 Who was the author of the book *101 Dalmatians*?

3 Who played *El Cid* on screen?

4 Was the character he played alive or dead at the end of the film?

5 Who directed the 1962 film *Lawrence of Arabia*?

6 Who starred as Lawrence?

7 Which Egyptian actor made his international mark in the same film?

8 Which of these three did not star in the 1961 film *Guns of Navarone*: David Niven, Gregory Peck, John Wayne?

9 Which actor led the seven in *The Magnificent Seven*?

10 Who directed *The Apartment*?

11 What was America's zaniest TV comedy show?

12 Who sang *Two Little Boys*?

13 Jan and Dean had a US number one in 1963; was its title a) *Surf City* b) *Surf with the Sharks* or c) *Surfing Smurfs*?

14 Which British comedian killed himself in Australia in 1968?

15 Which writers had worked on his radio and TV shows?

ANSWERS

15, Alan Simpson and Ray Galton

11, *Rowan and Martin's Laugh-In* 12, Rolf Harris 13, a) *Surf City* 14, Tony Hancock

6, Peter O'Toole 7, Omar Sharif 8, John Wayne 9, Yul Brynner 10, Billy Wilder

1, The Everly Brothers 2, Dodie Smith 3, Charlton Heston 4, Dead 5, David Lean

SPORT

. . . .

1 Which Swedish tennis player was born on 22 August 1964?

2 What cricketing first did Gary Sobers achieve in August 1968?

3 Against which team was he playing?

4 And who was bowling against him?

5 Why did South African cricketer Geoff Griffin have arm trouble?

6 What year?

7 Where?

8 What happened to him?

9 In which sport was the Eisenhower Trophy awarded?

10 Which Hungarian delighted Real Madrid fans in 1960?

11 Complete these 1960 tennis names: American Darlene …?

12 and South African Sandra …?

13 Which new Cup were English soccer clubs competing for in 1960?

14 Which golfer had his own "Army" of fans?

15 What was Karl Schranz's sport?

. . . .

ANSWERS

1, Mats Wilander 2, He hit six sixes in one over 3, Glamorgan 4, Malcolm Nash 5, He was called (no-balled) for throwing 6, 1960 7, In England, during the South African tour 8, He retired next year 9, Golf 10, Ferenc Puskas 11, "Hard 12, Reynolds 13, The League Cup 14, Arnold Palmer ("Arnie's Army") 15, Skiing

WORLD EVENTS

. . . .

1 Who was Dr Robert Soblen?

2 Which country sent a U2 spy plane over China?

3 What happened to it?

4 In which country was ZAPU campaigning?

5 What were its aims?

6 What did ZAPU stand for?

7 Who made a "first in 100 years" trip by train in Italy?

8 In which country were Flemish speakers complaining of inequalities?

9 In which country was *Der Spiegel* published?

10 Which civil rights organization was founded in London?

11 Whose ships were heading for Cuba carrying missiles?

12 Which two leaders confronted each other at this time?

13 What action did the USA take?

14 What did Kennedy promise in return for a Russian climb-down?

15 What proof did the USA show that Soviet missiles were in Cuba?

. . . .

ANSWERS

1, A spy working for the USSR 2, Taiwan 3, It was shot down 4, Southern Rhodesia 5, Black majority rule and independence 6, Zimbabwe African People's Union 7, The pope 8, Belgium 9, West Germany 10, Amnesty International 11, Soviet ships 12, Kennedy and Khrushchev 13, A blockade of Cuba 14, Not to invade Cuba, and to lift the blockade 15, Air photo

SPORT
SOCCER

. . . .

1 Who won the 1962 World Cup final?

2 Whom did they beat?

3 The score?

4 Which 60s World Cup final went into extra time?

5 Which team was in both the 1960 and 1964 European championship finals?

6 Did they win both?

7 Which Portuguese club won the 1961 and 1962 European Cup?

8 Which Italian team broke its winning run in 1963?

9 Which Yugoslav team lost in the 1966 European Cup final?

10 To whom?

11 Who won the last European Cup of the decade (1969)?

12 Which Scottish club lost the 1961 European Cup-winners' Cup final?

13 Did they appear in another 60s final?

14 Which London club won the Cup-winners' Cup in 1965?

15 And which other English team lost in the same final the next year?

. . . .

ANSWERS

QUIZ 118
POT LUCK
1966

· ·

1 What did Shell find off Great Yarmouth in 1966?

2 Which horse won the Gold Cup for the third year running in 1966?

3 Which party won the 1966 British general election?

4 Who handed over power to Suharto?

5 And where was this?

6 What went up with a bang in Dublin?

7 Which writer, who died in 1966, refused to watch television?

8 Where did a British airliner crash in Japan in March 1966?

9 What were a British doctor's average earnings in the mid 60s?

10 Whose Lola failed in Indianapolis?

11 Which British organization raised its membership subscription in 1966, for the first time since it was formed in 1905?

12 How much was the new fee?

13 How much was a guinea?

14 Which city's name was changed to Kinshasa in 1966?

15 Whom did Frank Sinatra marry in July 1966?

· ·

ANSWERS

15. Mia Farrow
13. One pound and one shilling (21 shillings) 14, Leopoldville in the Congo
drop out when leading the Indy 500 in 1966) 11, The AA 12, Three guineas
7, Evelyn Waugh 8, On Mount Fuji 9, About £4000 10, Jackie Stewart's (he had to
column 2, Arkle 3, Labour 4, Sukarno 5, Indonesia 6, Nelson's Column
1, Oil!

ARTS & ENTERTAINMENT

. . . .

1 Which writer created the character of Alf Garnett on TV?

2 What was the name of the show in which he appeared?

3 Who played Alf Garnett?

4 What soccer team did Alf support?

5 Who played his son-in-law in the TV show?

6 And whose father-in-law was this actor later to become?

7 In which country was *Shindig* a top pop music show on TV?

8 Who sang *Go Now* in 1965?

9 Who had "lost that loving feeling" in 1965?

10 Who was their record producer on this hit?

11 Which singer's initials were P J?

12 And what happened to his trousers?

13 Who had a first in 1965 with *Catch The Wind*?

14 Which US group recorded *Mr Tambourine Man* in 1965?

15 And who had written and also recorded the song?

. . . .

ANSWERS

1, Johnny Speight 2, *Till Death Us Do Part* 3, Warren Mitchell 4, West Ham 5, Antony Booth 6, Tony Blair's 7, United States 8, The Moody Blues 9, The Righteous Brothers 10, Phil Spector 11, P J Proby's 12, They kept splitting on stage 13, Donovan 14, The Byrds 15, Bob Dylan

QUIZ 120
PEOPLE

. . . .

1 With which industry was Jean Muir associated?

2 What instrument did Daniel Barenboim play in concert?

3 Whose 1964 *Othello* aroused controversy?

4 Which 90s fashion designer was being brought up by Barnardo's in the 60s?

5 Who wrote *The Hotel in Amsterdam*?

6 To which actress was he married (later divorced)?

7 In which film did Peter O'Toole play a retiring schoolmaster?

8 Which professor had a law to do with time and work named after him?

9 What was the essence of his law?

10 What did Norman Parkinson do for a living?

11 On which island did he settle in 1963?

12 What did Roger Penrose look for in space?

13 Which famous World War II fighter was designed by Sidney Camm (died 1966)?

14 Who wrote *Beyond Belief*, an account of the Moors Murders?

15 Which National Hunt jockey rode his first winner in 1969?

. . . .

ANSWERS

15, John Francome
11, Tobago 12, Black holes 13, The Hurricane 14, Emlyn Williams
to fill the time available for its completion 10, He was a photographer
6, Jill Bennett 7, *Goodbye Mr Chips* 8, Cyril Northcote Parkinson 9, Work expands
1, Fashion 2, Piano 3, Laurence Olivier 4, Bruce Oldfield 5, John Osborne

QUIZ 121
WORLD EVENTS
1962

. . . .

1 Where was King Saud the ruler?

2 In which country was the Vassall spy trial?

3 How had William Vassall been trapped into being a spy?

4 Where did Vassall work?

5 Which country attacked India in November 1962?

6 Which ex First Lady died in November this year?

7 Who had been her husband?

8 Who had become known as the Black Pimpernel?

9 Who were to be linked by a "hot line"?

10 Which US missile was being bought for the British navy?

11 From where was it launched?

12 Which French soldier escaped the firing squad?

13 Of which secret army had he been leader?

14 Where was this organization based?

15 And who had been its main target?

. . . .

ANSWERS

QUIZ 122
ARTS & ENTERTAINMENT

. . . .

1 Which composer included a part for tape recorder in his 1969 Stimmung ?

2 Complete the composer's names: Hans Werner…

3 Elliott…

4 Thea…

5 Harrison…

6 What instrument did John Ogden play?

7 Which conductor, famous for composing *West Side Story*, was working with the New York Philharmonic Orchestra in 1969?

8 Who wrote a musical work called *The Children's Crusade*?

9 Which Israeli actor starred in *Fiddler On The Roof*?

10 For what style of music was Loretta Lyn acclaimed?

11 James Galway played which instrument?

12 Coleman Hawkins died in 1969; was he a jazzman, a classical musician, or a pop drummer?

13 And what instrument did he play?

14 On which instrument was Gary Burton a virtuoso?

15 Who wrote a work called *Celtic Requiem*?

. . . .

ANSWERS

1, Karlheinz Stockhausen 2, Henze 3, Carter 4, Musgrave 5, Birtwistle 6, Piano 7, Leonard Bernstein 8, Benjamin Britten 9, Topol 10, Country music 11, Flute 12, A jazzman 13, Tenor saxophone 14, Vibraphone 15, John Taverner

QUIZ 123
POT LUCK

. . . .

1 Of which kingdom did Faisal become ruler in November 1964?

2 What title was given to Princess Margaret's son, born in 1961?

3 Who was Tatum O'Neal's actor father?

4 Who was George Walker's boxing brother?

5 Which Romanian gymnast was born in November 1961?

6 What was Surtsey?

7 And where did it appear in 1963?

8 Which famous father died in November 1969?

9 Which road tunnel eased cross-Thames traffic in 1963?

10 Which soccer player scored his 1000th goal in 1969?

11 Where is the Verrazano-Narrows Bridge, opened in 1964?

12 Which German tennis star was born on 22 November 1967?

13 What tragic event happened on that same date in 1963?

14 What was unusual about the new power station on the River Rance in France (1966)?

15 Which European queen died in November 1962?

. . . .

ANSWERS

15, Wilhelmina of the Netherlands
13, The assassination of President Kennedy 14, It was operated by tidal power
9, The Dartford Tunnel 10, Pele 11, New York 12, Boris Becker
6, A volcanic island 7, It came out of the sea off Iceland 8, Joseph Kennedy
1, Saudi Arabia 2, Viscount Linley 3, Ryan O'Neal 4, Billy 5, Nadia Comaneci

QUIZ 124
PEOPLE

. . . .

1 For whom did Tommy Lawrence play in goal?
2 Whose first symphony was premiered in 1968 when he was only 16?
3 Who wrote *The Ghost In The Machine*?
4 Which poet wrote *The Whitsun Weddings*?
5 What was the profession of Denys Lasdun?
6 With which university was he associated professionally?
7 And with which theatre?
8 Which criminal twins went to jail for a long, long time in 1969?
9 Which opera singer's real name was Kalogeropoulos?
10 With which event was Lt William Calley's name linked?
11 What did Sarah Caldwell do?
12 Which tough guy actor retired in 1961 (though he later came back)?
13 Which Civil Rights leader took up Martin Luther King's mantle in 1968?
14 Which 7ft 2 inch basketball star made his name at UCLA?
15 Which was his first professional team?

. . . .

ANSWERS

15, Milwaukee Bucks
conductor 12, James Cagney 13, Ralph Abernathy 14, Kareem Abdul-Jabbar
10, The My Lai massacre in Vietnam 11, She was an American orchestral
6, East Anglia 7, The National, in London 8, The Krays 9, Maria Callas
1, Liverpool 2, Oliver Knussen 3, Arthur Koestler 4, Philip Larkin 5, Architect

QUIZ 125
SPORT
SOCCER

. . . .

1 Who were English League champions in 1960?

2 Which East Anglian club surprised the soccer world in 1962 by winning the Championship?

3 How many times did Man Utd win the championship in the 60s?

4 Which team did the "double" in 1961?

5 Who won the 1969 English First Division title?

6 Which year did an Edinburgh club win the Scottish League?

7 How many championships did Rangers win in the decade?

8 And how many did Celtic win?

9 Which was Celtic's first winning year?

10 What year did Celtic win the Scottish Cup final 4-0?

11 Beating whom?

12 How many Scottish Cups did Rangers win in the 60s?

13 What was the score in the 1968 European Cup Final?

14 Who did they beat?

15 What was the score at 90 minutes?

. . . .

ANSWERS

1, Burnley 2, Ipswich 3, Twice (1965,1967) 4, Tottenham Hotspur 5, Leeds 6, 1960, Hearts 7, Three 8, Four 9, 1966 10, 1969 11, Rangers 12, Five 13, 4-1 (to Man Utd) 14, Benfica 15, 1-1

PEOPLE

. . . .

1 Was Bella Abzug a) a feminist b) a trombone player or c) a TV cook?

2 Which cartoonist created the Addams Family?

3 Who starred as Butch Cassidy in 1969?

4 Was he playing a real-life outlaw?

5 Who played his partner?

6 And the partner's name in the film?

7 For what was Francis Bacon famous a) painting b) writing c) singing?

8 Of which country was Nnamdi Azikiwe first president?

9 What year was that?

10 Who wrote The Edible Woman (1969)?

11 What nationality was this author?

12 For what was Charles Atlas famous?

13 Who was head of Desilu Productions?

14 Which author wrote Another Country?

15 Was he American, British or Australian?

. . . .

ANSWERS

1.a) 2, Charles Addams 3, Paul Newman 4, Yes 5, Robert Redford 6, The Sundance Kid 7, a) 8, Nigeria 9, 1963 10, Margaret Atwood 11, Canadian 12, His body-building courses 13, Lucille Ball 14, James Baldwin 15, American

QUIZ 127
ART & ENTERTAINMENT

1 From which university city did the Spencer Davies Group emerge in the 60s?

2 Which member of the Rolling Stones died in 1969?

3 How did he die?

4 Who had replaced him earlier that year?

5 Which band had a hit with a song called *5-4-3-2-1*?

6 Who was the first lead singer with this band who went on to a solo career?

7 Which famous guitarist formed Blind Faith along with Ginger Baker, Steve Winwood and Rick Grech?

8 Which group sang *Get Back*?

9 This *Old Heart of Mine* was a 1969 hit for … who?

10 Who sang *Where Do You Go To My Lovely*?

11 Who sang *Boom bang-a-bang* in 1969?

12 In which prestigious song-fest?

13 Why did the BBC ban a song by Jane Birkin and Serge Gainsbourg in 1969?

14 What was the song called?

15 *Those Were The Days* was a hit for which singer?

ANSWERS

QUIZ 128
POT LUCK

. . . .

1 Who was the world's first heart transplant recipient, in 1967?

2 How long did he survive?

3 In 1969 a sixth Nobel Prize was added; for what?

4 Which famous US broadcaster and journalist died in New York on 11 December 1965?

5 For what vocal characteristic was actress Tallulah Bankhead (died 1968) renowned?

6 Which British short story writer and novelist died in France in 1965?

7 The writer of the BIlly Bunter stories died in 1961. Who was he?

8 Which motorway bridge was opened in 1966?

9 Which New York nightspot became famous for twisting the night away?

10 Who recorded the *Revolver* album?

11 How did singer Jim Reeves die in 1964?

12 How many Gibb brothers were in the Bee Gees?

13 Name them.

14 Who were Scott, John and Gary?

15 Were the Walker brothers really brothers?

. . . .

ANSWERS

1. Louis Washkansky 2. 18 days 3. Economics 4. Ed Murrow 5. Her deep voice 6. Somerset Maugham 7. Frank Richards 8. The Severn bridge carrying the M4 9. The Peppermint Lounge 10. The Beatles 11. In a plane crash 12. Three 13. Barry, Maurice, Robin 14. The Walker Brothers 15. No

QUIZ 129
ENTERTAINMENT
STAR TREK

1 Who was the producer and inspirer of *Star Trek*?

2 Who was the first commander of the starship "Enterprise", in a pilot show?

3 Who took over the role for the TV series

4 What name was his character given?

5 In which country was this actor born?

6 Which *Star Trek* actor had earned the nickname "the male Fay Wray"?

7 Why?

8 Who played Scotty?

9 Was this actor American, Scottish or Canadian?

10 Who wrote a book entitled *I Am Not Spock*?

11 In the series, was he a Vulcan, a Vegan or a Klingon?

12 What part did De Forest Kelley play in the series?

13 Whose nickname was ...?

14 What part was played by George Takei?

15 Which member of the crew was played by Nichelle Nichols?

ANSWERS

QUIZ 130
PEOPLE

. . . .

1 Which business was Balenciaga a big name in?

2 Which jazz artist recorded *Take Five*?

3 Who wrote *Life At The Top*?

4 Which funny man's real name was Melvin Kaminsky?

5 Which spoof secret agent TV series did he help to create in 1962?

6 What was Edgar Bergen's act?

7 What was the name of his stage partner?

8 Which US comedian played the violin?

9 What was his theme tune?

10 What was his real name?

11 Which comedian was known as Uncle Miltie to his fans?

12 Which rock guitarist and singer was freed from jail in 1964?

13 Who sang that he'd left his heart in San Francisco?

14 What did Belmonte (died 1962) do for a living?

15 Who broke his record in the 60s?

. . . .

ANSWERS

1, Fashion 2, Dave Brubeck 3, John Braine 4, Mel Brooks 5, *Get Smart* 6, He was a ventriloquist 7, Charlie McCarthy 8, Jack Benny 9, *Love In Bloom* 10, Benjamin Kubelsky 11, Milton Berle 12, Chuck Berry 13, Tony Bennett 14, He was a bullfighter 15, El Cordobes

QUIZ 131
SPORT
1960

1 In which tournament final did Spurs beat a Spanish club 5-1?

2 Who were the Spanish team?

3 Which West Indian batsmen batted nearly 10 hours against England in 1960?

4 How did Bev Risman change codes?

5 Which soccer club were nicknamed "The Posh"?

6 What did it get into at last in 1960?

7 Which Scottish club lost the 1960 Cup Final to Rangers 2-0?

8 Which English club reached the final of the Inter City Fairs Cup in 1960, but lost?

9 Which club did Denis Law leave to join Manchester City in 1960?

10 Which sport's league collapsed before the 1961 season?

11 For whom did Neil Fox score 20 points in the Rugby League Cup Final of 1960?

12 Whom did Wolves beat in the 1960 FA Cup Final?

13 The score?

14 Of whom did Jock Stein become manager in 1960?

15 Who was the brains behind Lotus cars?

ANSWERS

1. European Cup-winners' Cup (1963) 2. Athlético Madrid 3. Sobers and Worrell 4. He switched from Rugby Union to Rugby League 5. Peterborough United 6. The Football League 7. Kilmarnock 8. Birmingham City 9. Huddersfield Town 10. British League ice hockey 11. Wakefield Trinity 12. Blackburn Rovers 13. 3-0 14. Dunfermline 15. Colin Chapman

WORLD EVENTS

1963

• •

1 Which Leonardo masterpiece went on show in Washington?

2 Where was the Mekong delta?

3 Who said "non" to Britain?

4 What reasons did he give?

5 Which body organ was successfully transplanted by surgeons in Leeds?

6 What post did John Profumo hold in the British government?

7 Which spy went missing in Beirut?

8 Which African federation collapsed?

9 What was the name of the US submarine which sank in April 1963?

10 Who was chosen to succeed Adenauer in West Germany?

11 With what achievement was he credited?

12 Who became an honorary American citizen this year?

13 Which European leader was voted president for life?

14 Which Alabama state governor was in the news for defying the Federal government?

15 On what date was President Kennedy assassinated?

• •

ANSWERS

1, The Mona Lisa 2, Vietnam 3, De Gaulle (over EEC membership) 4, Britain was not "continental" enough, being too close to its Commonwealth partners 5, A kidney 6, Minister of War 7, Kim Philby 8, The Central African Federation 9, "Thresher" 10, Ludwig Erhard 11, An economic miracle 12, Winston Churchill 13, Tito of Yugoslavia 14, George Wallace 15, 22 November

QUIZ 133
PEOPLE

. . . .

1 Which big band played at Kenendy's inauguration?

2 What was the bandleader's full name?

3 Clyde Beatty, who died in 1965, worked with what kinds of animals?

4 Which French writer wrote *The Prime of Life*?

5 *Happy Days* was a play by … whom?

6 Was Harry Blackstone a) a magician b) a scientist or c) a politician?

7 Who provided Bugs Bunny's voice?

8 Which hit show did Jerry Bock and Sheldon Harrick create?

9 What nationality was Sergei Bondarchuk?

10 What did he do?

11 With what revolution was Norman Borlaug associated?

12 The "It" girl died in 1965; who was she?

13 In which country was Ben Bella deposed in 1965?

14 Who was Daisy Bates?

15 What did Jean-Paul Belmondo do?

. . . .

ANSWERS

1. Count Basie 2. William Basey 3. Lions and tigers (in circuses) 4. Simone de Beauvoir 5. Samuel Beckett 6. a) A magician 7. Mel Blanc 8. *Fiddler On The Roof* 9. Russian 10. Film director 11. The green revolution in farming 12. Clara Bow 13. Algeria 14. An American Civil Rights activist 15. He was an actor

QUIZ 134
SCIENCE & TECHNOLOGY

. . . .

1 In space jargon what was an RV?

2 Who was the second Soviet man in space?

3 Date of his flight?

4 How many times did he orbit the Earth?

5 How many people went into space aboard "Voskhod 1" (1964)

6 Which President told Americans they were going to the Moon?

7 In which part of the Apollo spacecraft did the astronauts live?

8 What was the LEM?

9 What did it do?

10 What was the "Agena"?

11 And what part did it play in space exploration?

12 Whom did cosmonaut Tereshkova marry?

13 Which happy event pleased scientists?

14 What was ESO?

15 Where was it situated?

. . . .

ANSWERS

1, A rendezvous 2, Herman Titov 3, August 6, 1961, 4, 17 5, Three 6, Kennedy 7, The command module 8, The Lunar Excursion Module 9, It flew down to land on the Moon 10, A US rocket 11, It was used as a target in docking experiments 12, Fellow-cosmonaut Andrian Nikolayev 13, The couple had a daughter (having apparently suffered no ill effects from their space flights) 14, The European Southern Observatory 15, Chile

QUIZ 135
POT LUCK

1. What according to a 1960 TV advert were "you never alone with"?
2. What royal TV first took place in 1960?
3. In which country was Para Handy set?
4. Who narrated *Tales of the Riverbank*?
5. Who played Cathy Gale?
6. In which TV show?
7. Who spoke Churchill's words in *The Valiant Years*?
8. Which doctor did Richard Chamberlain play?
9. Who played Dr Gillespie in this show?
10. Who played Reg the foreman in *The Rag Trade*?
11. And what was the name of the fashon firm he worked for?
12. In which show did Fred and Wilma meet Barney and Betty?
13. In which series did Bill Simpson play a young doctor?
14. And who played Dr Cameron?
15. What was the first name of the doctors' housekeeper?

ANSWERS

QUIZ 136
WORLD EVENTS
1963

• •

1 Which east African country held its first independent elections in May 1963?

2 Who was elected premier?

3 Where did 10,000 people die in a cyclone?

4 Which country said it was pulling its navy out of NATO?

5 Why was Birmingham, Alabama, in the news?

6 In which city did Kenya's first National Assembly open?

7 Who expressed "fatherly pride" in Russia's first female cosmonaut?

8 Where were fanatical mullahs opposing the Shah?

9 Which mullah was arrested in June 1963 for opposing votes for women?

10 Which organization was founded in Addis Ababa in 1963?

11 For what was Oleg Penkovsky sentenced to death in Moscow?

12 Which 88-year-old declared he would retire as an MP?

13 Which constituency did he represent?

14 What accident had he suffered in 1962?

15 Who visited his "ancestral home" in Wexford in 1963?

• •

ANSWERS

1, Kenya 2, Jomo Kenyatta 3, Pakistan 4, France 5, Race troubles 6, Nairobi
7, Nikita Khrushchev 8, Iran 9, Khomeini 10, The Organization for African Unity
11, Spying for the West 12, Sir Winston Churchill 13, Woodford in Essex
14, He broke his leg while on holiday 15, President Kennedy

QUIZ 137
PEOPLE

• •

1 Who wrote the novel *Herzog* (1966)?

2 Harry Belafonte was still a big star; in which city was he born?

3 Vanessa Bell died in 1961; whose sister was she?

4 Who was known as "Soul Brother No. 1"?

5 What instrument did Julian Bream play?

6 This French poet who died in 1966 was a founder of surrealism; who was he?

7 Which star American footballer left the gridiron in 1966 for the movies?

8 Which US comic was refused entry to Britain in 1963?

9 Which critic and scholar wrote of "two cultures"?

10 Whose first novel was *Call For The Dead* (1961)?

11 What was his real name?

12 Which group sang *Stairway to Heaven*?

13 Which Dracula starred as a mad monk in 1965?

14 Who wrote how he'd "walked out one midsummer morning"?

15 What year was his book published?

• •

ANSWERS

1, Saul Bellow 2, New York 3, Virginia Woolf's 4, James Brown 5, Guitar 6, André Breton 7, Jim Brown 8, Lenny Bruce 9, C P Snow 10, John Le Carré 11, David John Moore Cornwell 12, Led Zeppelin 13, Christopher Lee 14, Laurie Lee 15, 1969

QUIZ 138
ARTS & ENTERTAINMENT

. . . .

1 In which TV show did John Alderton star as a teacher?

2 Who presented *Civilization* on British television?

3 Which writer/comedian starred in his own TV series, Marty?

4 Walter Gropius died in 1969; for what was he famous?

5 Where was he born?

6 With what school in architectural history is he associated?

7 What did Chet Huntley and David Brinkley do on American TV?

8 Who directed the 1961 film *The Misfits*?

9 The author of *From Here to Eternity*, he wrote The Thin Red Line (1961). Who was he?

10 On which BBC radio show did the Beatles drop in for a chat in June 1966?

11 Who was this show's presenter?

12 Which British DJ began his career in 1967 doing breakfast shows from out at sea?

13 What was the name of his pirate radio ship?

14 What did *What Did You Know* become in 1967?

15 What did Reginald Bosanquet do on TV?

. . . .

ANSWERS

POT LUCK

. . . .

1 In which series did Jeff Tracy's five sons star?

2 What were the five names?

3 After whom were they named?

4 What did 1960 TV ads tell people to go to work on?

5 From which Beatles album did *Michelle* come?

6 Which group recorded it and reached number one in 1966?

7 Which town did the Troggs come from?

8 Under what name did Mary O'Brien sing her way to the top?

9 Can you name her first hit single?

10 How many nervous breakdowns are there in a famous 1966 Rolling Stones song title?

11 Who sang *As Tears Go By*?

12 Which film was originally going to be called *Eight Arms To Hold You*?

13 Who was James Marcus Smith?

14 How did he wear his hair?

15 Who had a 1960 hit with *Love Is Like A Violin*?

. . . .

ANSWERS

1, Thunderbirds 2, Scott, Virgil, Alan, Gordon and John? 3, The first US astronauts 4, An egg 5, *Rubber Soul* 6, The Overlanders 7, Andover 8, Dusty Springfield 9, *I Only Want To Be With You* 10, Nineteen 11, Marianne Faithfull 12, *Help!* 13, P J Proby 14, In a pigtail 15, Ken Dodd

QUIZ 140
PEOPLE

. . . .

1 Whose last film was the 1965 movie *Ship of Fools*?

2 Which prehistoric human ancestor was discovered in 1961?

3 For what artform was Alexander Calder known?

4 Was he American or British?

5 Who founded his own airline in 1966?

6 Whose book *Over To Me* upset the cricket authorities?

7 Where was Fulham goalkeeper Tony Macedo born?

8 Which spy died in 1963 in Russia?

9 Which author with the same surname wrote *Tremor of Intent* in 1966?

10 Founder of Moral Re-Armament, he died in 1961. Who was he?

11 To which president was McGeorge Bundy an aide?

12 Which American Carol had her own TV show from 1967?

13 Of which country was Forbes Burnham leader?

14 Who starred as Henry VIII in *Anne of the Thousand Days*?

15 Which future President entered the US Congress in 1967?

. . . .

ANSWERS

1. Vivienne Leigh 2. Homo habilis or "handy man" 3. Sculpture 4. American 5. Freddie Laker 6. Jim Laker 7. Gibraltar 8. Guy Burgess 9. Anthony Burgess 10. Frank Buchman 11. Kennedy 12. Carol Burnett 13. Guyana 14. Richard Burton 15. George Bush

QUIZ 141
ARTS & ENTERTAINMENT

1 For what was Ivy Compton-Burnett honoured in 1962?

2 Who was the female human star of the film *One Million Years BC*?

3 Who played Alfie on screen?

4 And who sang the theme song from this film?

5 Who wrote the book on which *Born Free* was based?

6 Which animals featured in the film?

7 Who were the human co-stars?

8 Which US comedian died of a drugs overdose in 1966?

9 Which popular radio programme for children ended in 1961?

10 Which ever-cheerful broadcasting bandleader died in 1969?

11 What was his catchphrase?

12 In which sport had he continued competing until the age of 50?

13 Which TV show made Patrick Macnee famous?

14 And who starred alongside him as Emma Peel?

15 Which Galsworthy saga held TV audiences chairbound?

ANSWERS

1. Her work as a novelist 2. Raquel Welch 3. Michael Caine 4. Cilla Black 5. Joy Adamson 6. Lions 7. Bill Travers and Virginia McKenna 8. Lenny Bruce 9. Children's Hour 10. Billy Cotton 11. Wakey Wakey! 12. Motor racing 13. The Avengers 14. Diana Rigg 15. The Forsyte Saga

WORLD EVENTS

1963

- -

1 With which callgirl had Russian naval attaché Eugene Ivanov had an affair?

2 Which government minister admitted that he had lied about her?

3 What was Dr Stephen Ward's profession?

4 What role had he played in the Profumo affair?

5 How did he die?

6 What was to be new on Britain's roads?

7 Where was President Carlos Monray overthrown?

8 Which two Communist leaders danced together to show they were pals?

9 Which country introduced a 50 mph speed limit?

10 Who was named as the "third man" in the Burgess and Maclean spy scandal?

11 How widespread was the 1963 nuclear test ban treaty?

12 Which countries signed the treaty?

13 Which nuclear power refused to sign it?

14 Which robbery shocked Britain in August 1963?

15 What was special about the train?

- -

ANSWERS

1, Christine Keeler 2, John Profumo 3, Osteopath 4, He was a go-between and party organizer 5, He took a drugs overdose 6, Continental-style road signs 7, Ecuador 8, Tito and Khrushchev 9, Britain 10, Kim Philby 11, It covered tests in space, under water and in the atmosphere 12, USA, USSR and United Kingdom 13, France 14, The Great Train Robbery 15, It was a travelling post office, carrying banknotes on their way to the incinerator

QUIZ 143
ARTS & ENTERTAINMENT

....

1 Which Western marshal did James Arness play in *Gunsmoke*?

2 Whom did Eamonn Andrews talk to in bed in 1969?

3 Born Spangler Arlington Brough, this movie star died in 1969. What was his screen name?

4 Which country produced the crime series *Division 4* ?

5 Which brothers hosted a US TV Comedy Hour?

6 Who was the star of the "Lucy" TV shows?

7 Lew Stone (died 1969) was a famous a) bandleader b) actor or c) painter?

8 Who starred in the 1964 film *The Bargee*?

9 Which of the two Ronnies also appeared in this film?

10 Who starred in the film *An American Dream* (1966)?

11 Who wrote the book with the same title?

12 *Cash McCall* was a 1960 comedy starring … which leading man?

13 In which Western series did this actor later become a TV favourite?

14 Which actor played Bronco in a Western series of the same name?

15 Complete the name of this TV series: *Have Gun* …

....

ANSWERS

PEOPLE

• •

1 Whose most famous book was *Tobacco Road*?

2 What was the title of his 1962 novel?

3 Which comedian closed the show with "Say goodnight, Gracie"?

4 Who was Gracie?

5 What year did their partnership end?

6 Who wrote the screenplay for the 1965 film *What's New Pussycat*?

7 To which country was Walter Annenberg appointed ambassador?

8 From?

9 Which Italian film director made *The Red Desert*?

10 Was Sir Edward Appleton, who died in 1965, a scientist, a racehorse trainer, or an actor?

11 What had he studied in particular?

12 Who was Eddie Arcaro, who retired in 1961?

13 Who sang *Make The World Go Away* in 1965?

14 Which country did Vladimir Ashkenazy flee in 1963?

15 What musical instrument did he play?

• •

ANSWERS

QUIZ 145
POT LUCK

. . . .

1 Who sang "Yellow Submarine" on the Beatles' track?

2 Brian and Carl Wilson were two of the ....?

3 Which group hit the top in 1967 with *I'm A Believer*?

4 Who wrote this song?

5 Who was the only non-American Monkee?

6 What was the theme song from the 1967 film *Countess of Hong Kong*?

7 Who wrote it?

8 Who sang it in four languages?

9 What were the languages?

10 What name did Gerry Dorsey adopt?

11 What had he in common with Cliff Richard?

12 Who recorded a French version of *The Last Waltz*?

13 What nationality was Françoise Hardy?

14 And Richard Anthony?

15 Whose first number one hit song was *Massachusetts*?

. . . .

ANSWERS

1. Ringo Starr 2. Beach Boys 3. The Monkees 4. Neil Diamond 5. Davy Jones 6. *This Is My Song* 7. Charlie Chaplin 8. Petula Clark 9. French, Italian, German and (lastly) English 10. Engelbert Humperdinck 11. They were both born in India 12. Mireille Mathieu 13. French 14. Also French 15. The Bee Gees

QUIZ 146
PEOPLE

. . . .

1 Which science fiction writer wrote *Opus 100* (1969)?

2 On which instrument was Larry Adler a virtuoso?

3 Which playwright wrote *Who's Afraid Of Virginia Woolf*?

4 What nationality was the writer Chinua Achebe?

5 Who retired as director of the Royal Institution in 1966?

6 Where was he born?

7 Of what study was he a pioneer?

8 Who was the author of the 1962 novel *Flesh*?

9 Which former Australian prime minister died in 1967?

10 Which Ray Bradbury book was filmed in 1963?

11 What nationality was scientist Niels Bohr?

12 Who sang *I Can't Stop Loving You*?

13 Who had a US number one (his last) with *Why*?

14 For what was Daniel Cohn-Bendit famous?

15 In which country was he active?

. . . .

ANSWERS

1. Isaac Asimov 2. Harmonica 3. Edward Albee 4. Nigerian 5. Sir Lawrence Bragg 6. Australia 7. Crystallography 8. Brigid Brophy 9. Stanley Bruce (Viscount Bruce) 10. *Fahrenheit 451* 11. Danish 12. Ray Charles 13. Frankie Avalon 14. He was a student activist and would-be revolutionary 15. West Germany

POT LUCK

• •

1 Who made a TV film called *The Magical Mystery Tour*?

2 Who took over from Paul Jones as Manfred Mann's lead singer?

3 Who backed Wayne Fontana?

4 Where did windsurfing first catch on?

5 Was it an American invention?

6 Had Scrabble been invented in 1960?

7 How about Trivial Pursuit?

8 Whose boyfriend was Ken in 1961?

9 How long had Lego been on sale in 1960?

10 Who wrote about Adam Dalgleish?

11 What was his job?

12 What was his literary hobby?

13 How did Sid James get his battered features?

14 Where was he born?

15 Who was accused of being a "soft" Home Secretary?

• •

ANSWERS

SPORT
1960

· ·

1 Where did Lotus win their first Grand Prix in 1960?

2 Who was the driver?

3 Which Australian fast bowler called it a day in 1960?

4 Where did he play his last Test?

5 In what event did Dorothy Hyman win a silver for Britain in the Rome Olympics?

6 Which boxer dazzled in the light-heavyweight division at the Rome Games?

7 Which New Zealander won the 5000 metres gold in Rome?

8 In which event did Ralph Boston set a 1960 world record?

9 What was Bill Bradley's sport?

10 Which event did he win for the second year running in 1960?

11 How many goals did Jimmy Greaves score against West Brom in Dec 1960?

12 Who was 1960 motor racing world champion?

13 Which country produced Maria Bueno?

14 What sport was played at Odsal Stadium?

15 For whom did Richie Benaud bowl?

· ·

ANSWERS

1, Monaco 2, Stirling Moss 3, Ray Lindwall 4, Calcutta 5, 100 metres 6, Cassius Clay 7, Murray Halberg 8, Long jump 9, Cycling 10, The Tour of Britain 11, Five 12, Jack Brabham 13, Brazil 14, Rugby League 15, Australia

QUIZ 149
ARTS & ENTERTAINMENT

. . . .

1 Which Italian directed *Romeo and Juliet* at the Old Vic?

2 In which musical did Ron Moody play Fagin?

3 Which D H Lawrence novel sold out?

4 Who made a film of the same novelist's *Sons and Lovers*?

5 Who wrote the play *Rhinoceros*?

6 And who starred in a 1960 production of it in London?

7 What happens to all but one of the characters in this play?

8 Who wrote *The Caretaker*?

9 How many characters were there in this play?

10 Who wrote *Billy Liar*?

11 And which actor appeared on stage as Billy?

12 Which film of 1960 had given this actor his first big hit?

13 Who wrote the novel on which this film was based?

14 And who played the female lead in the film?

15 In which city was the film set?

. . . .

ANSWERS

QUIZ 150
MUSIC

. . . .

1 Which singer did The Band back?

2 From which country did all but one of The Band come?

3 Whick folk singer had a hit with *There But For Fortune*?

4 Whose *Barbara Ann* was a hit of 1966?

5 Which was the Beach Boys' first UK number one?

6 On which label were Beatles abums issued in the USA?

7 What was their first US album?

8 Who replaced Eric Clapton as guitarist with the Yardbirds?

9 How did the Bee Gees get their name?

10 Who sang *Nadine* (1964)?

11 How many albums did the "super-group" Blind Faith release?

12 What was it called?

13 Which US singer came to the fore in 1963 with *Fingertips*?

14 How old was he then?

15 From which disability had he suffered since birth?

. . . .

ANSWERS

1, Bob Dylan 2, Canada 3, Joan Baez 4, The Beach Boys 5, *Good Vibrations* 6, Capitol 7, *Introducing the Beatles* 8, Jeff Beck 9, From Barry Gibbs' initials 10, Chuck Berry 11, One 12, *Blind Faith* 13, Stevie Wonder 14, 13 15, Blindness

POT LUCK

· ·

1 What sport did Barry John excel in?

2 Who began his career with a group called Bluesdoggy?

3 Which future TV host and journalist arrived in London from Sydney in 1962?

4 Whose first thriller was *Cover Her Face*?

5 Of which "feathery-sounding" pop group was David Crosby a member?

6 In which scandal was Stephen Ward involved?

7 Who wrote a book called *The Trial of Stephen Ward*?

8 Who married Katharine Worsley in 1961?

9 What title was given to their first son, born 1962?

10 Of which subject was Nicholas Kaldor a professor?

11 Which musical instrument did Eileen Jones play?

12 Was Melanie Klein (died 1960) a) folk singer b) a judge or c) a psychoanalyst?

13 Which Scottish-born Hollywood actress retired from movies in 1969?

14 Complete the title: *Joseph and the* …

15 What was John Lennon's middle name?

· ·

ANSWERS

1, Rugby Union football 2, Elton John 3, Clive James 4, P D James 5, The Byrds 6, The Profumo affair 7, Ludovic Kennedy 8, The Duke of Kent 9, The Earl of St Andrews 10, Economics 11, Piano 12, c) A psychoanalyst 13, Deborah Kerr 14, *Amazing Technicolor Dreamcoat* 15, Winston

QUIZ 152
ARTS & ENTERTAINMENT

- -

1 Which British comedian lent his name and wit to radio's *Round the Horne*?

2 Augustus John, who died in 1961, was famous as …a) painter b) poet c) Rugby player?

3 Which satirical revue was performed by Bennett, Miller, Cook and Moore?

4 Can you complete the names of the four stars?

5 Which controversial programme about nuclear holocaust was banned by the BBC in 1966?

6 Was *Bonanza!* a TV Western, a show about oil prospectors, or a series about the Alaskan gold rush?

7 Which TV character arrived by Tardis?

8 Which actor was the first to play this character?

9 Who were the aliens out to exterminate him?

10 In which part of the British Empire was the play *Conduct Unbecoming* set?

11 Who took Julie Andrews' stage role in the film of *Camelot*?

12 Playing which Queen?

13 Which British actor made his name in a1969 production of *The Resistible Rise of Arturo Ui*?

14 Which king of Wessex was played by David Hemmings on screen in 1969?

15 Who played dancer Isadora Duncan on screen?

- -

ANSWERS

1, Kenneth Horne 2, a) Painter 3, *Beyond the Fringe* 4, Alan Bennett, Jonathan Miller, Peter Cook, Dudley Moore 5, *The War Game* 6, A Western 7, Dr Who 8, William Hartnell 9, Daleks 10, India 11, Vanessa Redgrave 12, Guinevere 13, Leonard Rossiter 14, Alfred the Great 15, Vanessa Redgrave

QUIZ 153
SPORT

. . . .

1 In which event did Don Thompson win Olympic gold in 1960?

2 Who was Britain's first £100-a-week soccer player?

3 Which country's rugby players were known as Springboks?

4 Where did the 1961 Giants play baseball?

5 Who was the youngest century-maker in test cricket?

6 For whom did he play?

7 Who managed Ipswich Town soccer club to win the Second Division title in 1961?

8 Who was elected president of FIFA in 1961?

9 For whom did Tom van Vollenhoven play Rugby League in 1961?

10 In which sport was Azam Khan British Open champion?

11 Which new technology revolutionized pole vaulting in 1961?

12 Who beat Christine Truman to win Wimbledon in 1961?

13 How much did Spurs pay to sign Jimmy Greaves from Milan in Dec 1961?

14 Who was the Spurs manager who did the deal?

15 How many goals did Greaves score on his Spurs debut?

. . . .

ANSWERS

1, 50 km walk 2, Johnny Haynes 3, South Africa's 4, San Francisco 5, Mushtaq Mohammad 6, Pakistan 7, Alf Ramsey 8, Sir Stanley Rous 9, St Helens 10, Squash 11, Fibreglass poles 12, Angela Mortimer 13, £99,999 14, Bill Nicholson 15, Three

QUIZ 154
POT LUCK

....

1 Which future England soccer star and TV presenter was born in 1960?

2 What is Gary Lineker's middle name?

3 At which university did novelist David Lodge teach English?

4 What was Lord Lichfield good at?

5 Which future boxing champion was born in England in1965, later moving to Canada?

6 What year did Tim Rice meet his first musical partner?

7 Who was the partner?

8 Which entertainer ran Glasgow's Metropole Theatre?

9 Which US comedian was still entertaining the troops?

10 Which US comedian recorded a driving instructor's nightmare?

11 Which singing Andy had his own rocking chair on TV?

12 What subject did Hugh McIlvanney write about?

13 Who received 33,000 fan letters a month for playing a floppy haired Russian?

14 Which 1963 pop album's cover was photographed by theatrical snapper Angus McBean?

15 Which was recorded by …?

....

ANSWERS

1, Gary Lineker 2, Winston 3, Birmingham 4, Photography 5, Lennox Lewis 6, 1965 7, Andrew Lloyd Webber 8, Jimmie Logan 9, Bob Hope 10, Bob Newhart 11, Andy Williams 12, Sport 13, David McCallum (as Ilya Kuryakin in *The Man from UNCLE*) 14, *Please Please Me* 15, The Beatles

QUIZ 155
SCIENCE & TECHNOLOGY

. . . .

1 Which famous German company had just started making aircraft again in 1960?

2 Was Erwin Schrodinger (died 1961) a famous chemist, geologist or physicist?

3 And what nationality was he?

4 On what was Dr Benjamin Spock an expert?

5 Whose behaviour was blamed on parents adopting his theories?

6 Who wrote *Theory of Superconductivity* (1964)?

7 What was "Syncom" (1963)?

8 What were "splashdowns"?

9 What happened to the Mercury 4 space capsule in 1961?

10 Who was the astronaut?

11 What made "Gemini 3" (1965) important for the Americans?

12 Which American first walked in space?

13 What year?

14 What record did "Gemini 7" set in 1965?

15 Who were the astronauts?

. . . .

ANSWERS

QUIZ 156
ARTS & ENTERTAINMENT

- **1** Who starred as Queen Eleanor in *The Lion in Winter*?
- **2** Complete the film title: *Bonnie and …*?
- **3** *Village of the Damned* was a sci-fi film; on which book was it based?
- **4** Author?
- **5** In which TV series did George have a daughter called Mary and a son-in-law called Andy?
- **6** On whose plays was the TV series *The Age of Kings* based?
- **7** Who starred in the TV Western series *Wells Fargo*?
- **8** Who was the presenter of BBC TV's *Panorama*?
- **9** Which was the most famous TV puppet series, featuring Lady Penelope?
- **10** Which former child star had a 61 hit with *Sailor*?
- **11** In which language had this song first appeared?
- **12** Which well-known British singer also recorded this song?
- **13** Who starred in *The Power Game*?
- **14** Who played the wagon boss in *Wagon Train*?
- **15** Which German couple took TV viewers under the sea to view the wildlife?

ANSWERS

1, Katharine Hepburn 2, *Clyde* 3, *The Midwich Cuckoos* 4, John Wyndham 5, *Dixon of Dock Green* 6, Shakespeare's 7, Dale Robertson 8, Richard Dimbleby 9, *Thunderbirds* 10, Petula Clark 11, German 12, Anne Shelton 13, Patrick Wymark 14, Ward Bond 15, Hans and Lotte Hass

MUSIC

THE BEATLES

. . . .

1 Which instrument did Stuart Sutcliffe play with the original Beatles?

2 Whom did Ringo replace as the group's drummer?

3 In which German city did the Beatles make a name?

4 By what name had the group first been known?

5 On whose 1961 German records did they provide backing?

6 Which was their first UK record to enter the Top 20?

7 How high it did it get?

8 Who became the Beatles' manager in 1961?

9 What year did Beatles records occupy number 1–5 on the US chart?

10 Which was their first album?

11 On which label was it issued?

12 Complete these two Beatles' song titles: *Can't Buy Me …*

13 *Stawberry …*

14 Name the Beatles' second album

15 And the last album they issued in the 60s?

. . . .

ANSWERS

1, Bass 2, Pete Best 3, Hamburg 4, The Quarrymen 5, Tony Sheridan 6, Love Me Do 7, 17 8, Brian Epstein 9, 1964 10, Please Please Me 11, Parlophone 12, Love 13, Fields Forever 14, With The Beatles 15, Abbey Road (1969)

QUIZ 158
POT LUCK

1 In which business was John Major getting his first work experience?

2 Baron Marks died in 1964; whose son was he?

3 On which sport did Harry Carpenter commentate?

4 Of which annual event was John Snagge the broadcast voice?

5 Who wrote *A House for Mr Biswas* (1961)?

6 Which veteran actress appeared in *Charlie Girl* (1965)?

7 Which tycoon bought the *News of the World* in 1969?

8 He founded Morris Motors, and died in 1963 as Lord …?

9 In which city was his company's Cowley motor plant?

10 Was Conor Cruise O'Brien a diplomat or a short story writer?

11 With which TV show was Arthur Negus associated?

12 Which travel writer wrote *Slowly Down The Ganges* (1966)?

13 What sports event did Psidium win in 1961?

14 What had he been?

15 What did his wife do in 1963?

ANSWERS

1, Banking 2, Michael Marks, co-founder of Marks and Spencer 3, Boxing (mostly) 4, The University Boat Race 5, V S Naipaul 6, Anna Neagle 7, Rupert Murdoch 8, Nuffield 9, Oxford 10, A diplomat and later an Irish politician 11, *Going For A Song* 12, Eric Newby 13, The Derby 14, A spy for the Soviet Union 15, She followed him to Russia (but came back in 1965)

QUIZ 159
WORLD EVENTS

• •

1 Who missed his party's conference because of illness?

2 What announcement did he make from hospital?

3 Whom did Conservative friends say had been kept out by a "magic circle"?

4 Who became Britain's new prime minister?

5 Of which country did Ben Bella become president?

6 Which southeast Asian federation was created in September 1963?

7 Where was President Morales deposed?

8 Whom did the UN vote to refuse admission to?

9 Which race did the Russians say they wouldn't join?

10 Who won an election at Kinross to win his first seat in the Commons?

11 Where was the Ba'athist government overthrown?

12 Who gave up his title to become Mr Hogg?

13 Which play opened the new National Theatre in London?

14 Who played the Dane?

15 Who was the "little sparrow" who died in 1963?

• •

ANSWERS

1, Harold Macmillan 2, His resignation as prime minister 3, R A B Butler, the favourite to succeed Macmillan 4, Lord Home 5, Algeria 6, Malaysia 7, Honduras 8, China 9, The race to the Moon 10, Alec Douglas-Home (Lord Home before he gave up the title) 11, Iraq 12, Lord Hailsham 13, *Hamlet* 14, Peter O'Toole 15, Edith Piaf

MUSIC

• •

1 Which singer was born David Robert Jones in 1947?

2 What was his first hit (1969)?

3 Who sang *Turn! Turn! Turn!*?

4 Whose song about a Wichita lineman was a 1968 hit?

5 What name did a Californian musician called Don Van Vliet adopt in 1964?

6 How many Carpenters were there?

7 Who recorded a song called *Bits And Pieces*?

8 Whose first band was called the Roosters?

9 Where was Jimmy Cliff born?

10 Where was Joe Cocker born?

11 With which song did he reach the top in 1968?

12 *Three Steps to Heaven* was a hit by … who?

13 How had this singer died shortly before the record's release?

14 Was he British or American?

15 Who sang with the Commodores?

• •

ANSWERS

1, David Bowie 2, *Space Oddity* 3, The Byrds 4, Glen Campbell 5, Captain Beefheart 6, Two 7, The Dave Clark Five 8, Eric Clapton 9, Jamaica 10, Sheffield 11, *With a Little Help From My Friends* 12, Eddie Cochran 13, He was fatally injured in a car accident 14, American 15, Lionel Richie

QUIZ 161
WORLD EVENTS
1964

. . . .

1 Who said he would run for President against Johnson?

2 Whose sultan lost his throne?

3 In which African state did soldiers mutiny over low pay?

4 What opened at Innsbruck in Austria in January 1964?

5 Whose ship "Voyager" was sunk?

6 Where were Tutsi and Hutu killing each other?

7 What was Britain planning to built five of for its navy?

8 On which island were Greeks and Turks up in arms?

9 Where did George Papandreou win an election in 1964?

10 Who declared Paris fashions "out of date"?

11 King Paul died in March 1964: king of where?

12 Who succeeded him?

13 Which queen gave birth to her third son this year?

14 Who fought on the beaches of England?

15 What was abolished to become part of Britain's Ministry of Defence?

. . . .

ANSWERS

15. The Admiralty
10. Mary Quant 11. Greece 12. Constantine 13. Elizabeth II 14. Mods and rockers
5. The Australian Navy 6. Rwanda 7. Polaris submarines 8. Cyprus 9. Greece
1. Barry Goldwater 2. Zanzibar's 3. Uganda 4. The Winter Olympics

POT LUCK

. . . .

1 Which jockey enjoyed a partnership with trainer Noel Murless until 1966?

2 What was this jockey's nickname?

3 What name was newborn boxer-to-be "Barry" McGuigan given in 1961?

4 Who played Dr Roger Corder on television?

5 Who was "our man at St Mark's"?

6 In which nautical radio series did he also appear?

7 What did British TV weathermen use for the first time in 1962?

8 Whose soup can pictures amused some critics?

9 Which veteran actresses starred in *Whatever Happened to Baby Jane?*

10 Which Beatle met his wife while filming in 1964?

11 Who was she?

12 Which 18th-century book was declared obscene in London in 1964?

13 What did *The Daily Herald* become in 1964?

14 Who wrote the play *Entertaining Mr Sloane*?

15 Who sang *There I've Said It Again*?

. . . .

ANSWERS

1, Lester Piggott 2, The Long Fellow 3, Finbar 4, Herbert Lom 5, Leslie Phillips 6, *The Navy Lark* 7, Celsius temperatures 8, Andy Warhol 9, Joan Crawford and Bette Davis 10, George Harrison 11, Patti Boyd 12, Fanny Hill 13, *The Sun* 14, Joe Orton 15, Bobby Vinton

QUIZ 163
PEOPLE

· ·

1 Which singer had a hit with *Ramblin' Rose*?

2 *Songs From A Room* was an album by which songwriter?

3 Who sang *Twistin the Night Away*?

4 How many members had Cream?

5 Who were they?

6 Alan, Merrill, Wayne and Jay were the original … who?

7 At which theme park did they first play?

8 And on whose TV show did they make their name?

9 Who was the younger brother who joined in 1966?

10 Who were black America's answer to the Osmonds?

11 Which Japanese artist moved to New York to be a conceptual artist and film-maker?

12 Whose *In Dreams* was a 1963 hit?

13 Who starred in the film *The Shoes of the Fisherman* (1968)?

14 In which film did he play a Greek?

15 Who wrote the original novel *The Shoes of the Fisherman*?

· ·

ANSWERS

1, Nat "King" Cole 2, Leonard Cohen 3, Sam Cooke 4, Three 5, Eric Clapton, Ginger Baker and Jack Bruce 6, The Osmonds 7, Disneyland 8, Andy Williams' 9, Donny 10, The Jackson Five 11, Yoko Ono 12, Roy Orbison 13, Anthony Quinn 14, *Zorba the Greek* 15, Morris West

QUIZ 164
SPORT

. . . .

1 Which English soccer club signed Ian St John from Motherwell?

2 Which German racing driver died in a 1961 crash at Monza?

3 What position did Wally Grout occupy in the Australian cricket team?

4 How many Tests did Peter May play as England captain?

5 Who replaced Accrington Stanley in the Football League in 1962?

6 Which Aston Villa player signed for Inter Milan in 1961?

7 Which rugby player was known as "Monsieur Le Drop"?

8 For which country did Richard Sharp play rugby?

9 Which cricket match was played for the last time in 1962?

10 Which former England captain became manager of Arsenal?

11 Which former Test bowler became an England Test selector in 1962?

12 What brought most outdoor sport in Britain to a halt in 1962?

13 What idea did football pools promoters dream up to solve the problem?

14 Whom did Australia beat in the 1962 Davis Cup final?

15 What car did Graham Hill drive to become world champion?

. . . .

ANSWERS

1, Liverpool 2, Wolfgang von Trips 3, Wicket keeper 4, 41 5, Oxford United 6, Gerry Hitchens 7, Pierre Albaladejo of France 8, England 9, Gentlemen v Players 10, Billy Wright 11, Alec Bedser 12, The big freeze that winter 13, The pools panel forecasting "results" 14, Mexico 15, BRM

QUIZ 165
WORLD EVENTS
1964

. . . .

1 Who did not deny at his trial that he had planned sabotage?

2 Where was Colonel Nasser in power?

3 Whom did he vow to expel from the Arab world?

4 Which disease closed schools in Aberdeen?

5 Who became prime minister of Southern Rhodesia in 1964?

6 Who did he replace?

7 What new development was planned around Bletchley in England?

8 On which island were Finns, Irish, Swedes and Canadians trying to keep the peace?

9 Where did Prince Phouma lose his job as head of government?

10 Where was Jigme Dorji assassinated?

11 Which Asian leader died of a heart attack in May 1964?

12 Who succeeded him as prime minister?

13 What was the B-70 revealed in the USA?

14 What did Khrushchev help push a button to start in Egypt?

15 What did the Pope say women must not use?

. . . .

ANSWERS

ARTS & ENTERTAINMENT

1 What were the Everly brothers' first names?

2 Who was the elder?

3 Their 1961 hit *Walk Right Back* had a "death song" on the flip side; its title?

4 Who wrote Cliff Richard's 1960 hit *I Love You*?

5 Who played bass guitar with The Shadows in 1960?

6 David Spencer had brief fame as a "one hit wonder", – under what name?

7 Roy Orbison had a middle name; what was it?

8 On which Italian song was Elvis' *It's Now Or Never* based?

9 Who played piano on many Presley hits?

10 And who were his vocal backing group?

11 From which film did the 1961 hit *Wooden Heart* come?

12 Which German bandleader co-wrote this song?

13 He also wrote a bestseller for Sinatra; which one?

14 To which group fid Captain Cephas Howard and Canon Colin Bowes belong?

15 And who was the group's lead singer?

ANSWERS

1, Don and Phil 2, Don (born 1937) by two years 3, *Ebony Eyes* 4, Hank Marvin and Bruce Welch 5, Jet Harris 6, Ricky Valance 7, Kelton 8, *O Sole Mio* 9, Floyd Cramer 10, The Jordanaires 11, *GI Blues* 12, Bert Kampfaert 13, *Strangers In The Night* 14, The Temperance Seven 15, Whispering Paul McDowell

POT LUCK

1963

· ·

1 Which TV show told viewers "the weekend starts here!"?

2 Which comedian starred in *Taxi!*?

3 Were the Telegoons real people or puppets?

4 Which TV show did Ray Martine host?

5 Which San Francisco landmark closed its doors in 1963?

6 The 10th anniversary of his death was unremarked by the Kremlin; who was he?

7 Which horse won the 1963 Grand National?

8 Where was President Fuentes overthrown?

9 How did Patsy Cline die?

10 Where?

11 Whose jets fired at a US ship?

12 Which country supplied the planes?

13 Which new airliner took to the skies in February 1963?

14 Which royal cancelled a visit to France?

15 Which banknote was new in Britain?

· ·

ANSWERS

1. *Ready Steady Go!* 2. Sid James 3. Puppets 4. *Stars and Garters* 5. Alcatraz 6. Stalin 7. Ayala 8. Guatemala 9. In an air crash 10. Tennessee 11. Cuba's 12. USSR 13. Boeing 727 14. Princess Margaret 15. £5

QUIZ 168
WORLD EVENTS
1964

. . . .

1 Where was Nelson Mandela imprisoned in June 1964?

2 Who were greeted by 300,000 fans in Australia?

3 Why did National Guardsmen appear on the streets of New York in July 1964?

4 Which central African state became independent to the sound of bagpipes?

5 How many new people were being born each year, according to the UN?

6 Which was the most populous country in the mid 60s?

7 How many Chinese were there?

8 Where was US destroyer "Maddox" attacked in 1964?

9 How did the US respond?

10 Who was beginning the campaign trail across America for the Democrats?

11 Who resigned as US Attorney General?

12 Why?

13 Where did Indonesian paratroops land?

14 Which new British strike plane made its first flight in September 1964?

15 What was its eventual fate?

. . . .

ANSWERS

1, Robben Island 2, The Beatles 3, To quell race riots 4, Malawi 5, 64 million 6, China 7, About 600 million 8, The Gulf of Tonkin, off Vietnam, 9, Air strikes were made from carriers 10, Lyndon Johnson 11, Robert Kennedy 12, He was to run for the Senate 13, Malaysia 14, The TSR-2 15, It was cancelled

QUIZ 169
SPORT
SOCCER

1 Who was in goal for Spurs when they won the FA Cup in 1967?

2 Which later Wimbledon manager was in the same Cup-winning side?

3 For whom did Chris Lawler play ?

4 Alex Young and Colin Harvey played in which 60s team?

5 Who became England's most costly centre-forward when he joined Chelsea from Aston Villa in 1966?

6 His son also achieved success as a striker; his first name?

7 Which soccer club did Brian Clough join as a player in 1961?

8 Which balding Scot moved from Dundee to Spurs in 1964?

9 Who became Britain's most expensive goalkeeper when he joined West Ham from Kilmarnock in 1967?

10 Which goalkeeping brothers swopped clubs in 1966?

11 Paul Reaney and Billy Bremner played for which English soccer club?

12 What nationality was Leeds soccer star Albert Johanneson?

13 McLintock, Neill and Simpson all played for?

14 How about Mick Channon and Terry Paine?

15 For whom did Gordon Banks keep goal after leaving Leicester City?

ANSWERS

MUSIC

. . . .

1 In which country were the pop group Love formed in 1965?

2 With which group did John Mayall play from 1962?

3 He sang *Misty* wherever he appeared; who was he?

4 What were Simon and Garfunkel's first names?

5 With which song did they hit the charts in 1966?

6 Which of them had previously recorded as Arty Garr?

7 Their second hit was written in England in 1966; title?

8 Which of their songs featured in the film *The Graduate*?

9 Whose *Strangers in the Night* topped charts everywhere?

10 Did he have any other number one hits in the 60s?

11 What was his next biggest-seller in the UK?

12 Which future superstar of pop was born in Detroit in 1961 with the surname Caccione?

13 With whom was Barry Manilow working as an arranger for his TV shows in 1967?

14 Whose *Dock of the Bay* was a 1968 hit?

15 Who had a smash with *He'll Have To Go in* 1960?

. . . .

ANSWERS

1, USA 2, Bluesbreakers 3, Johny Mathis 4, Paul Simon and Art Garfunkel 5, *The Sounds of Silence* 6, Garfunkel 7, *Homeward Bound* 8, *Mrs Robinson* 9, Frank Sinatra 10, No 11, *My Way* (No. 5, in 1969) 12, Madonna 13, Ed Sullivan 14, Otis Redding 15, Jim Reeves

QUIZ 171
POT LUCK

....

1 Where was premier Kassim overthrown in 1963?

2 Where was Fidel the leader?

3 Where did Mount Agung volcano erupt in 1963?

4 Which TV programme was retitled *The Power Game*?

5 What was BBC TV's new science show in 1964?

6 Who played General Allenby in the film *Lawrence of Arabia*?

7 With what industry was Sir Frederick Handley Page associated?

8 In which musical did Elaine Page appear in 1969?

9 What subject was Michael Palin studying at university?

10 On what was Reginald Passmore an expert?

11 The author of *Titus Groan* died in 1968. Who was he?

12 Which future political star became Labour MP for Plymouth in 1966?

13 Who played Gypsy Rose Lee's mother in a film?

14 What was the film?

15 What did Gypsy Rose Lee do?

....

ANSWERS

1. Iraq 2. Cuba (Castro) 3. Bali 4. *The Plane Makers* 5. *Tomorrow's World*
6. Jack Hawkins 7. Aviation 8. *Hair* 9. History 10. Nutrition 11. Mervyn Peake
12. Dr David Owen 13. Rosalind Russell 14. *Gypsy* 15. She was a stripper

QUIZ 172
WORLD EVENTS
1964

. . . .

1 Which Kremlin fixture found himself removed while on holiday?

2 Where was he on holiday?

3 Who succeeded him as Communist Party boss?

4 And who was the new Soviet prime minister?

5 How did 57 people flee to the West from East Berlin in October 1964?

6 Which African government told Britain it was going to declare UDI?

7 What did UDI stand for?

8 Who was awarded the 1964 Nobel Peace Prize?

9 Which country exploded its first nuclear bomb in 1964?

10 Why was this a surprise to some?

11 How many seats did Labour win in the 1964 general election?

12 Why was this election called?

13 How many days of dynamic action did prime minister Wilson promise?

14 What had played a major part in the campaign, for the first time in Britain?

15 Who declared cheerfully "Brothers, we are in our way"?

. . . .

ANSWERS

1, Nikita Khrushchev 2, The Black Sea 3, Leonid Brezhnev 4, Alexei Kosygin 5, They tunnelled beneath the Wall 6, Southern Rhodesia 7, Unilateral Declaration of Independence 8, Martin Luther King 9, China 10, Some experts said it would be the 70s before China had an A-bomb 11, 317 12, Labour's majority had shrunk to two, 13, 100 days 14, Television and advertising techniques 15, George Brown

QUIZ 173
POT LUCK

. . . .

1 Who was director of Armagh Planetarium in1965?

2 Which comedians appeared in *The Riviera Touch*?

3 Who wrote *The Human Zoo*?

4 Where did Lady Mountbatten die in 1960?

5 Which musician received an honorary knighthood in 1965?

6 Where was he born?

7 Which veteran actor, known by his initials, died in 1960?

8 Who was Britain's Chancellor of the Exchequer from 1962–64?

9 In which sport was Colin Ingleby-Mackenzie a character?

10 For work in which field did Sir Peter Medawar win the 1960 Nobel Prize for medicine?

11 Who wrote an opera called *Taverner*?

12 Who was Celtic's captain in the 1967 European Cup final?

13 For which newspaper did Magnus Magnusson work from 1961–67?

14 Which ballerina became a Dame in 1963?

15 What was her real name?

. . . .

ANSWERS

1, Patrick Moore 2, Morecambe and Wise 3, Desmond Morris 4, Borneo 5, Yehudi Menuhin 6, New York 7, A E Matthews 8, Reginald Maudling 9, Cricket 10, Immunology 11, Peter Maxwell Davies 12, Billy McNeill 13, *The Scotsman* 14, Alicia Markova 15, Alice Marks

QUIZ 174
ARTS & ENTERTAINMENT

1 Runaway singer, real name Charles Westover; stage name?
2 Which Beatles song did he cover in 1963?
3 In which country was Cliff Richard born?
4 When Tony Meehan left the Shadows, who replaced him on drums?
5 Who backed Marty Wilde?
6 In which TV serial did actor-singer John Leyton appear as Ginger?
7 Which British girl singer had a 1961 hit when only 14?
8 What was the title of her first record?
9 In 1963 this same singer topped the bill on tour. Who were the supporting group?
10 Which 1962 film was retitled in the USA as *It's Great To Be Young*?
11 Who was the star?
12 Which singer struck gold in 1962 with *I Remember You*?
13 Born in Coventry, he'd emigrated to … where?
14 What was distinctive about his style?
15 Can you name his follow-up hit?

ANSWERS

1, Del Shannon 2, *From Me To You* 3, India 4, Brian Bennett 5, The Wildcats
6, *Biggles* 7, Helen Shapiro 8, *Please Don't Treat Me Like A Child* 9, The Beatles
10, *The Young Ones* 11, Cliff Richard 12, Frank Ifield 13, Australia 14, He yodelled
15, *Lovesick Blues*

QUIZ 175
SPORT

. . . .

1 Did Fred Winter ride on the flat or in National Hunt races?

2 Whom did Dick Tiger beat to become world middleweight champion in 1962?

3 Which veteran did Cassius Clay beat in four rounds in Nov 1962?

4 Who was the first bowler to take 250 Test wickets (1962)?

5 Where did he achieve the feat?

6 For which cricketing country did Neil Harvey star?

7 Why was golfer Bob Charles unusual?

8 How long did it take Liston to knock out Patterson in 1963?

9 Who declared in 1963 that England would win the World Cup next time?

10 Who won the first world netball championship (1963)?

11 Who had his arm fractured by West Indian Wes Hall but batted next day?

12 By what surname did Billie Jean first make a name in tennis?

13 Which horse won the 1963 Derby?

14 In which sport was Mickey Wright 1963's most successful female?

15 Who captained Yorkshire to the county cricket title in 1963?

. . . .

ANSWERS

1, National Hunt 2, Gene Fullmer 3, Archie Moore 4, Fred Trueman 5, In Christchurch, New Zealand 6, Australia 7, He played left-handed 8, 130 seconds 9, Alf Ramsey 10, Australia 11, Colin Cowdrey 12, Moffitt 13, Relko 14, Golf 15, Brian Close

WORLD EVENTS

1964

• •

1 Who was sent packing by American voters in the presidential contest of 1964?

2 Which party had chosen him?

3 Who replaced his brother as ruler of Saudi Arabia?

4 Who gave his jewelled tiara to the world's poor?

5 Whose currency was on the slide ?

6 Which train-cutter got his marching orders in December 1964?

7 Whose paratroops entered Stanleyville to protect hostages?

8 Where was Stanleyville?

9 Where was "Zond 2" headed?

10 What did British MPs vote to abolish?

11 Which African leader was known as "Burning Spear"?

12 Which country did he lead?

13 Whose 400th anniversary was being celebrated in Britain and around the world in 1964?

14 Which town was at the heart of Shakespeare events?

15 Which city was attacked by Russian tanks in August 1968?

• •

ANSWERS

QUIZ 177
POT LUCK

. . . .

1 In which sport was Willie Mays named "Player of the Decade"?

2 Which army hats reached the top of the US charts in 1966?

3 What was found in a garden in Norwood, South London?

4 Who played Rita in *Till Death Us Do Part*?

5 What was the TV show that the BBC made as a spin-off from Z Cars?

6 What kind of police organization did it describe?

7 Which Dublin monument was blown up?

8 Which event brought Llyn Davies European gold in 1966?

9 Who became the BBC's first cricket correspondent in 1963?

10 In which 60s year was the first classic radio serial *Journey Into Space* set?

11 Which 60-second radio panel game started in 1964?

12 Who was Billy Graham?

13 What did the Warlocks become in 1965?

14 Who was their lead guitarist?

15 Which famous musical-show songwriter died in 1960?

. . . .

ANSWERS

1. Baseball 2. The Green Berets 3. The World Cup 4. Una Stubbs 5. *Softly Softly* 6. A Regional Crime Squad 7. Nelson's Column 8. Long jump 9. Brian Johnston 10. 1965 11. *Just A Minute* 12. He was an American evangelist 13. The Grateful Dead 14. Jerry Garcia 15. Oscar Hammerstein II

QUIZ 178
MUSIC

1 In which town was Marty Robbins in 1960?

2 Who appeared in *Expresso Bongo*?

3 Who led Blues Incorporated?

4 Which embryo group emerged from this early 60s line up?

5 From which group was Ian Stewart dropped for "looking too normal"?

6 Who replaced Brian Jones in the Rolling Stones?

7 Where did Keith Richard and Mick Jagger first meet?

8 Whose album was *Got Love If You Want It*?

9 Who was the Linda of Linda and the Stone Poneys?

10 In which US city was Diana Ross born?

11 Which group did she leave in 1969?

12 Who fronted the Hoochie Coochie Men?

13 By what name did Reginald Dwight later become famous?

14 Which 60s Faces singer was London-born but very Scottish?

15 Who sang *Mathew and Son* in 1967?

ANSWERS

QUIZ 179
SPORT

. . . .

1 Which 18-year-old took 100 wickets for Kent in 1963?

2 Who won the first one-day cup final at Lord's (1963)?

3 Why did Colin Meckiff have to give up cricket?

4 Which Irish player joined Leeds from Manchester United in Aug 1963?

5 Which new format was added to the Ryder Cup in 1963?

6 Who broke Australia's eight-year domination of Davis Cup in 1963?

7 Which horse beat the much-fancied Mill House in the 1963 Gold Cup?

8 Who followed Ted Dexter as England cricket captain in 1964?

9 For whom did Don Clarke kick goals?

10 Where was Sonny Liston when his 1964 fight with Muhammad Ali ended?

11 Why did Muhammad Ali change his name?

12 Who scored the fastest-ever goal in British soccer in 1964?

13 How fast was it?

14 Which former England left-half hung up his boots in 1964?

15 For which club had he made a record 764 League appearances?

. . . .

ANSWERS

1, Derek Underwood 2, Sussex 3, He was called for throwing 4, Johnny Giles 5, Fourballs 6, USA 7, Arkle 8, Mike Smith 9, New Zealand's Rugby Union team 10, On his stool 11, Black Muslims persuaded him Cassius Clay was a "slave name" 12, Jim Fryatt for Bradford PA against Tranmere Rovers 13, Four seconds 14, Jimmy Dickinson 15, Portsmouth

POT LUCK

1966

. . . .

1 With which car maker did BMC merge in 1966?

2 Which runner from Kansas set a new mile record in 1966?

3 For whom was Rattin playing when sent off at Wembley in 1966?

4 What was his offence?

5 André Breton died in 1966; was he a poet, a painter or a former French premier?

6 What were non-aligned nations?

7 How did George Blake escape from jail in 1966?

8 Which car company made the Interceptor?

9 What was the former name of Lesotho?

10 What were new on British letters from 1966?

11 What new model did Rootes introduce under the Hillman name in 1966?

12 Where was "Orbiter 2" circling in 1966?

13 Which city in Italy was hit by floods in 1966?

14 Which art gallery there suffered severe losses of records?

15 What was the "brain drain"?

. . . .

ANSWERS

1, Jaguar 2, Jim Ryun 3, Argentina 4, Arguing with the referee 5, A poet (and founder of Surrealism) 6, Those allied neither to West or East 7, He used a ladder made of rope and knitting needles 8, Jensen 9, Basutoland 10, Postcodes 11, The Hunter 12, The Moon 13, Florence 14, The Uffizi 15, The movement of British (and other) scientists to the USA

QUIZ 181
ARTS & ENTERTAINMENT

. . . .

1 From which 1963 film did the song *Bachelor Boy* come?

2 Starring?

3 Who recorded a tune called *Dance On!* in 1963?

4 And which girl singer did a vocal version?

5 In which film did Elvis Presley sing *Rock-A-Hula Baby*?

6 And which girl singer featured in *It's Trad Dad* (1961)?

7 Who recorded *Nut Rocker* in 1962?

8 Of which classical piece was it a revamp?

9 *Come Outside* was a novelty song in which a boy , sung by …?

10 Tried to chat up a girl, voiced by …?

11 She later appeared as Miss Brahms, in which comedy show?

12 And in later life appeared around Albert Square in …?

13 Which duo recorded *Diamonds* (1963)?

14 Wayward Wind was a 1963 follow-up hit; for which singer?

15 The Shadows were still going strong in March 63 with a) *Foot Tapper* b) *Head Banger* c) *Heart Breaker*?

. . . .

ANSWERS

1, *Summer Holiday* 2, Cliff Richard and The Shadows 3, The Shadows 4, Kathy Kirby 5, *Blue Hawaii* 6, Helen Shapiro 7, B Bumble and the Stingers 8, Tchaikovsky's *Nutcracker Suite* 9, Mike Sarne 10, Wendy Richard 11, *Are You Being Served?* 12, *EastEnders* 13, Jet Harris and Tony Meehan 14, Frank Ifield 15, a) *Foot Tapper*

SPORT

1964

- **1** What got Peter Swan, David Layne and Tony Kay into trouble in 1964?
- **2** Who was voted Europe's Footballer of the Year for 1964?
- **3** In what were Tony Nash and Robin Dixon gold medallists?
- **4** What sport did Ken Venturi star in?
- **5** Who became the youngest ever Cup Final player in 1964?
- **6** Playing for which team?
- **7** Did he end up on the winning side?
- **8** Which American driver won the French Grand Prix in 1964?
- **9** In what was Bernard Farrelly world champion in 1964?
- **10** How old was Scobie Breasley when he won the 1964 Derby?
- **11** Who won the 1964 Open golf championship?
- **12** Which sport allowed substitutes for the first time in 1964?
- **13** In which sport did Terry Downes win a world title?
- **14** Who ended Downes' career by stopping him in 1964?
- **15** Who was sacked as manager of Wolverhampton Wanderers in August 1964?

ANSWERS

1, They were accused of fixing soccer matches 2, Denis Law 3, Bobsled – 1964 Winter Olympics 4, Golf 5, Howard Kendall 6, Preston North End 7, No. West Ham won 3-2 8, Dan Gurney 9, Surfing 10, 50 11, Tony Lema 12, Rugby League 13, Boxing 14, Willie Pastrano 15, Stan Cullis

QUIZ 183
ARTS & ENTERTAINMENT

. . . .

1 Which was the first "Liverpool-sound" number one in the British charts?

2 By?

3 What was Gerry's surname?

4 His brother Fred was also a group member; true or false?

5 Who managed this group, and others even more famous?

6 What was the Beatles' first chart-topper?

7 Which British group sang *Sweets for My Swee*t?

8 Who were behind Billy J Kramer?

9 What was their first number one hit?

10 Which song took the Beatles to the top of the US charts in 1963?

11 Which Beatles song included the often repeated chorus "Yeah Yeah Yeah"?

12 Did Dave Clark play a) drums b) guitar or c) keyboards?

13 Name the 1963 film in which the Dave Clark Five appeared?

14 Whose first British hit was *The House of the Rising Sun* (1964)?

15 Name their lead singer.

. . . .

ANSWERS

QUIZ 184
POT LUCK

- -

1 Which sportsman's nickname was "Broadway Joe"?

2 In 1966, who sang These Boots Are Made For Walking?

3 Dedicated Follower of Fashion was a hit for ... who?

4 In which country was poet Peter Porter born?

5 Which future political heavyweight was working for the National Union of Seamen in 1968?

6 For which TV show did Allan Plater write many scripts?

7 Which Eastbourne doctor suspected of killiing his patients was reinstated by the Medical Council in 1961?

8 Who directed 2001– A Space Odyssey?

9 Which field marshal and adviset to Churchill died in 1963?

10 Who starred as the upwardly mobile student in The Graduate ?

11 Who flew into New York on Pan Am flight 101 in February 1964?

12 For what was Bill Brandt famous?

13 For what was Mancunian Joe Brown renowned?

14 What was BBC-2's first programme (1964)?

15 Who resigned in 1965 as leader of the Conservatives in Britain?

- -

ANSWERS

1, Joe Namath 2, Nancy Sinatra 3, The Kinks 4, Australia 5, John Prescott 6 Z Cars 7, John Bodkin Adams 8, Stanley Kubrick 9, Viscount Alanbrooke 10, Dustin Hoffman 11, The Beatles 12, Photographing nudes 13, Mountain climbing 14, Play School 15, Alec Douglas-Home

PEOPLE

. . . .

1 What name did the Strawberry Hill Boys switch to?

2 Who sang about people needing people in 1964?

3 Is that her real name?

4 In which city was she born?

5 In which musical did she play Fanny Brice?

6 Which US group sang *My Girl* in 1965?

7 Where was Peter Tosh born?

8 With which band did he sing in the 60s?

9 With which "underground" group was Lou Reed singing in 1966?

10 Junior Walker and the …?

11 Which lady was walking on by in 1964?

12 *Blowin' In The Wind* was a 1966 hit for who?

13 What kind of music did John Coltrane play?

14 On which instrument?

15 Who wrote the songs *Suzanne* and *Famous Blue Raincoat*?

. . . .

ANSWERS

1, The Strawbs 2, Barbara Streisand 3, Yes, though Barbara was spelt with the extra 'a' 4, New York 5, *Funny Girl* 6, The Temptations 7, Jamaica 8, The Wailers 9, The Velvet Underground 10, All Stars 11, Dionne Warwick 12, Steve Wonder 13, Jazz 14, Saxophone 15, Leonard Cohen

QUIZ 186
ARTS & ENTERTAINMENT

- -

1 Which girl group sang *Will You Love Me Tomorrow* in 1961?

2 What was Tommy Steele's biggest hit of 1960?

3 Complete this 1967 song title *I Was Kaiser Bill's ...*?

4 Who sang it?

5 *Simon Says* was a 1968 hit for which US group?

6 Which US singer recorded *What Becomes Of The Brokenhearted* (1966)?

7 Who warbled *Caterina* in 1962?

8 Who sang *Everyone's Gone To The Moon* (1965)?

9 Whose *Last Waltz* of 1967 became an end of evening classic?

10 Which bandleader had a hit with *African Waltz* in 1961?

11 Who was his singer, and wife?

12 Pepe and Pablo were sound-alike titles of records by which 60s pianist?

13 Which actor-singer sang *What Kind Of Fool Am I*?

14 *Even the Bad Times Are Good* was a 1967 hit for who?

15 Big in the 70s, they first showed in 1968 with Debora. Who are they?

- -

ANSWERS

1, The Shirelles 2, *What A Mouth* 3, *Batman* 4, Whistling Jack Smith 5, 1910 Fruitgum Co. 6, Jimmy Ruffin 7, Perry Como 8, Jonathan King 9, Engelbert Humperdinck 10, Johnny Dankworth 11, Cleo Laine 12, Russ Conway 13, Anthony Newley 14, The Tremeloes 15, T Rex

POT LUCK

. . . .

1 What were "happenings"?

2 Which US magazine called London the "swinging" city?

3 With which fashionable store was Barbara Hulanicki associated?

4 Where was John Stephen making his name, and money?

5 Which city was he born in: a) London b) New York c) Glasgow?

6 What were hipsters?

7 Which Eastern-style dress became fashionable for both sexes?

8 Which street in Chelsea was a magnet for "swinging" tourists and locals?

9 Who staged an anti-Vietnam War show called *US*?

10 What was the capital of Rhodesia?

11 Where was Donald Campbell killed in 1967?

12 Which Rolling Stones' song was banned from British TV?

13 Complete this slightly altered 60s phrase from an *Oz* cover : "Turn on, tune in …?

14 Who was Albert DeSalvo, a prison escapee in the USA?

15 Whom did teenage fans fight for a glimpse of at Heathrow in February 1967?

. . . .

ANSWERS

1, Artistic events of a way-out kind (such as silent music) 2, *Time* 3, Biba
4, Carnaby Street 5, c) Glasgow 6, Trousers fitted to the hips, rather than the
waist 7, The kaftan 8, The King's Road 9, Peter Brook and the RSC 10, Salisbury
11, Coniston Water 12, *Let's Spend the Night Together* 13, drop dead
14, The Boston Strangler 15, The Monkees

SPORT

1964

• •

1 Who won golf's first World Matchplay championship in 1964?

2 Where was the match played?

3 And which British player lost?

4 Which batsman became the first to score 100s against every Test country?

5 For whom did Jim Standen play soccer in 1964?

6 And what was his other sport in summer?

7 For?

8 Why was 1964 a good year for them?

9 Which landmark did Fred Trueman achieve in 1964?

10 Where were baseball's Cardinals from?

11 Which woman won her second successive US singles tennis title in 1964?

12 Which rider won his fourth Tour de France in succession in 1964?

13 Which English soccer club took the First Division title in 1964?

14 Who were European soccer champions, beating the USSR 2-1?

15 Which race did Team Spirit win in 1964?

• •

ANSWERS

1, Arnold Palmer 2, Wentworth 3, Neil Coles 4, Ken Barrington 5, West Ham 6, Cricket 7, Worcestershire 8, They won the county championship for the first time 9, His 300th Test wicket 10, St Louis 11, Maria Bueno 12, Jacques Anquetil 13, Liverpool 14, Spain 15, Grand National

WORLD EVENTS

1965

. . . .

1 Where did Sukarno rule?

2 What did he announce he might do about UN membership?

3 Which British foreign secretary resigned after losing a by-election?

4 Whose was the biggest-ever funeral, in terms of TV audience?

5 Where did the body of Sir Winston Churchill lie in state?

6 Whose government was led by Sean Lemass?

7 Which British territory was Spain trying to choke by blockade?

8 What was banned on British TV?

9 Was it still allowed in the press?

10 B-57 jets were in action over Vietnam; of which British plane were they a development?

11 What was the capital of North Vietnam?

12 In which US state was Selma, scene of a 1965 march by civil rights activists?

13 With which European state did Israel agree to diplomatic relations?

14 Where was Da Nang?

15 What was it?

. . . .

ANSWERS

1, Indonesia 2, He threatened to leave the UN 3, Patrick Gordon-Walker 4, Churchill's 5, Westminster Hall 6, The Irish Republic's 7, Gibraltar 8, Cigarette advertising 9, Yes 10, The Canberra 11, Hanoi 12, Alabama 13, West Germany 14, South Vietnam 15, A huge air base

QUIZ 190
PEOPLE

. . . .

1 What was Nathaniel Adams Coles' performing name?

2 Was Judy Collins a singer, a golfer or a racing driver?

3 What did Howard Cosell present on American television?

4 Which movie star was awarded a special Oscar in 1960, the year he died?

5 Who starred in *The Bill Cosby Show*?

6 In which secret agent comedy-drama did he also star?

7 Which TV first took place on Sunday 5 Ooctober 1969?

8 Who did the animations for this show?

9 Who was Grandma Moses?

10 How old was she when she died in 1961?

11 Who wrote the novel *A Severed Head*?

12 What subject did she teach at Oxford University?

13 Who starred as a gigolo in the film *Sweet Bird of Youth*?

14   In which industry was Stavros Niarchos a big player?

15 Who directed the film *The Odd Couple*?

. . . .

ANSWERS

QUIZ 191
ARTS & ENTERTAINMENT

. . . .

1. *The Night Has A Thousand Eyes* was a smash for which US singer in 1963?
2. Which singer fronted the Tremeloes in 1963?
3. Who appeared as Paul's grandfather in the Beatles' first film?
4. What was the film title?
5. Which comedian took the title song into the charts?
6. Which group sang *Do Wah Diddy Diddy*?
7. Which 1964 group featured a girl drummer named Honey?
8. Can you name their only hit record?
9. How many Pennies were there, singing *Juliet*?
10. Who took *Albatross* to the top of the charts in 1968?
11. Which US singer gloomily sang *It's Over*?
12. What was The Kinks' first number one hit?
13. How many UK number ones did Sandie Shaw have?
14. With which group did Judith Durham sing?
15. *Concrete and Clay* was a 1965 hit … for who?

. . . .

ANSWERS

QUIZ 192
PEOPLE

. . . .

1 For what was Lorin Maazel distinguished?

2 Was he American, Australian or French?

3 Which singer-writer gave us *Lonesome Cities* in 1968?

4 Which actress starred in the films of *Irma La Douce* and *Sweet Charity*?

5 With which black power group was Huey Newton associated?

6 Paul Muni died in 1967; was he an actor, writer or politician?

7 Where was Cardinal Mindszenty safe but unable to leave?

8 Whose real name was Norma Jean Mortensen?

9 In which country was the Rev Moon born?

10 For what form of art was Marcel Marceau famous?

11 Who was Larry Hagman's mother?

12 In which Broadway show did she make the "hills alive with …"?

13 Who was Dino Crocetti?

14 And who was his partner in the comedy films that helped establish their careers?

15 Which wartime German field marshal died in 1960?

. . . .

ANSWERS

1, Orchestral conductor 2, American 3, Rod McKuen 4, Shirley MacLaine 5, The Black Panthers 6, Actor 7, The US Embassy in Budapest 8, Marilyn Monroe 9, South Korea 10, Mime 11, Mary Martin 12, *The Sound of Music* 13, Dean Martin 14, Jerry Lewis 15, Kesselring

QUIZ 193
SPORT

. . . .

1 Who won the Rugby League cup in 1964?

2 Which yacht kept the America's Cup in the USA?

3 Where was the Shell Shield played for?

4 Who won the first Shell Shield in 1965?

5 For whom did Jim Parks play Test cricket?

6 What year did Liverpool first enter European soccer competition?

7 They were vanquished by a team coached by Helenio Herrera; which team?

8 For whom did Nobby Stiles play his club football?

9 Which soccer player was knighted on his retirement in 1965?

10 Which English soccer team was relegated to Division 2 in 1965, for the first time since 1932?

11 Who won the Greater Greensboro Open at the age of 52 in 1965?

12 Which rally driver passed his British driving test first time in 1965?

13 Who was the first European in 45 years to win the Indy 500 (1965)?

14 Which former boxer was found dead of gunshot wounds in London?

15 Which batsman was dropped by England in 1965 for being too slow?

. . . .

ANSWERS

1. Widnes 2, Constellation 3, West Indies 4, Barbados 5, England 6, 1965 7, Inter Milan 8, Manchester United 9, Stanley Matthews 10, Wolves 11, Sam Snead 12, Timo Makinen 13, Jim Clark 14, Freddie Mills 15, Ken Barrington

ARTS & ENTERTAINMENT

· ·

1   Which film featured the Beatles number *Ticket To Ride*?

2   Which group topped the charts with *Go Now* in 1964?

3   Whose sister was Tom Springfield?

4   What was her first big hit, in 1964?

5   Who sang *Say It With Flowers* in 1961?

6   *Elusive Butterfly* was a very 60s song, recorded in 1966 … but by whom?

7   *The Loco-Motion* was a dance hit for which US singer?

8   Hank Locklin had a top ten hit in 1960. Title?

9   Who recorded *Hey Joe* (1967)?

10   *But I Do* was a 1961 hit for a strangely named US vocalist … who?

11   *Ferry Across the Mersey* (1964) was sung by?

12   *Desafinado* was a rare jazz entry into the charts in 1864; by which musician?

13   What instrument did he play?

14   Another instrumental hit was *Stranger on the Shore* (1962). Who had this hit?

15   Which instrument featured on this hit?

· ·

ANSWERS

1, *Help!* 2, The Moody Blues 3, Dusty Springfield 4, *I Only Want To Be With You* 5, Dorothy Squires 6, Bob Lind 7, Little Eva 8, *Please Help Me I'm Falling* 9, Jimi Hendrix 10, Clarence "Frogman" Henry 11, Gerry and the Pacemakers 12, Stan Getz 13, Tenor saxophone 14, Acker Bilk 15, Clarinet

QUIZ 195
PEOPLE

1   Who said "I have a dream"?

2   What kind of books did Louis L'Amour write?

3   Which unsmiling silent screen comic died in 1966?

4   Was Paul Hindemith (died 1963) a composer, a scientist, or a writer?

5   What nationality was he?

6   Which former US President died in October 1964?

7   How old was he?

8   Which artist painted swimming pool pictures?

9   Where did he paint them?

10   What was Kirsten Flagstad famous for?

11   Who were Flatt and Scruggs who split in 1969?

12   Their full names?

13   Who was famous for conducting the Boston Pops Orchestra?

14   Who was Caryl Chessman?

15   What happened to him in May 1960?

ANSWERS

1, Martin Luther King 2, Westerns 3, Buster Keaton 4, A composer 5, German 6, Herbert Hoover 7, 90 8, David Hockney 9, California 10, Opera singing, especially Wagner 11, Country and western singers 12, Lester Flatt and Earl Scruggs 13, Arthur Fiedler 14, A US convict, sentenced to death 15, He was executed after years of legal battles and eight stays of execution

QUIZ 196
ARTS &
ENTERTAINMENT

. . . .

1 Who were Joe Brown's backing group?

2 What was their biggest 60s hit (1962)?

3 Which 60s song became Liverpool FC's anthem?

4 Who recorded it?

5 Who were the writers?

6 And which show had it featured in?

7 Who were Shane Fenton's backing group?

8 *I'm Alive* was a 1965 hit for which group?

9 Which comedian sang *Tears*?

10 Which group recorded *Keep on Running* (1966)

11 Who was this group's lead vocalist?

12 Which James Bond theme song was sung by Nancy Sinatra?

13 With which group did Reg Presley appear?

14 What was probably this group's best-known hit, though it only reached No. 2 in the charts?

15 When did a Stone sing on a Beatles' hit?

. . . .

ANSWERS

You Need Is Love
12, You Only Live Twice 13, The Troggs 14, Wild Thing 15, Mick Jagger sang on All
8, The Hollies 9, Ken Dodd 10, The Spencer Davis Group 11, Steve Winwood
Pacemakers 5, Rodgers and Hammerstein 6, Carousel 7, The Fentones
1, The Bruvvers 2, A Picture of You 3, You'll Never Walk Alone 4, Gerry and the

QUIZ 197
SPORT

. . . .

1 Who rode Sea Bird II to win the 1965 Derby?

2 Which golfer won the 1965 Open?

3 Which course was it played over?

4 Which ex-bank clerk from Sydney won his first major tennis title in 1965?

5 Which one

6 How did he get on at Wimbledon this year?

7 Making how many successive Wimbledon defeats?

8 In what year did Jack Nicklaus turn professional?

9 What did he call his own company?

10 In which sport was the Gillette Cup final contested?

11 Who said "the more I practise, the luckier I become"?

12 For whom did Jack Flavell play cricket?

13 Which 1965 contest between Britain and the USA finished 12-12?

14 For which country did David Watkins play Rugby?

15 Was Siggy Held a) a footballer b) a skater or c) a boxer?

. . . .

ANSWERS

1, Lester Piggott 2, Peter Thompson 3, Royal Birkdale 4, Fred Stolle 5, The French men's singles. 6, Beaten in final by Emerson 7, Three 8, 1961 9, Golden Bear 10, Cricket 11, Golfer Gary Player 12, Worcestershire 13, The Walker Cup golf match 14, Wales 15, a) A footballer for West Germany

QUIZ 198
SCIENCE & TECHNOLOGY

. . . .

1 What new pen arrived in 1963?

2 Which country invented it?

3 Who launched the first electronic typewriter?

4 What year?

5 On what was its memory stored?

6 Could people video the 1966 World Cup?

7 Could people listen to personal stereos by 1969?

8 What was the Phonovid of 1965?

9 Which sci-fi author wrote *Stranger In A Strange Land* (1965)?

10 What did the initials ICBM stand for?

11 Who flew in "Mercury 6"?

12 How many orbits did Gordon Cooper make during his 1963 space flight?

13 What did John Hayes Hammond (died 1965) invent?

14 What was PAL (1962)?

15 In which country was it developed?

. . . .

ANSWERS

1. The felt tip 2. Japan (Pentel) 3. IBM 4. 1965 5. Magnetic tape 6. No 7. No 8. An early video disc 9. Robert Heinlein 10. Inter Continental Ballistic Missile 11. John Glenn 12. 22 13. Radio remote control 14. A colour TV system 15. West Germany

SPORT
1966

• •

1 Who pulled on a red number 10 jersey for the first time in 1966?

2 What first did Roberta Gibb achieve in 1966?

3 Which duo managed Manchester City to promotion from Division 2 in 1966?

4 What position did Clive Rowlands play in rugby?

5 From which US state did tennis star Nancy Richey come?

6 Tommie Smith and Lee Evans were a) athletes b) racing drivers or c) soccer players?

7 Which former boxing champion shot himself in May 1966?

8 What were last used at the 1966 Commonwealth Games?

9 Where were the Games staged?

10 Who won the 1966 Indy 500 race?

11 What was new to punters on British racetracks in 1966?

12 Who won the first ever world softball championship in 1966?

13 Who beat Palmer to win the US Open of 1966?

14 Whose husband was Larry King?

15 How did she fare in the 1966 Wimbledon?

• •

ANSWERS

WORLD EVENTS

• •

1 What was the port of Hanoi?

2 Which Japanese car company was hoping to break into the British market?

3 Which British MP was knocked out in a brief boxing match?

4 Which American politician turned up in Moscow for a visit?

5 What kind of craft was "Molnya 1"?

6 Where was President Cabral ousted?

7 Whose troops landed to fight leftist guerrillas there?

8 Which British seaside town was the scene of teenage gang fights?

9 Whom did prime minister Wilson meet in Rome in April 1965?

10 To whom did Yashin and Puskas pay tribute in a farewell soccer match?

11 What heavy industry did British MPs vote to nationalise?

12 Whose "Lunar 5" failed to make a landing on the Moon?

13 Which European country did the Queen visit in May 1965?

14 At which historic meadow did Mrs Kennedy watch a memorial unveiled?

15 Which historic event had taken place there 750 years before?

• •

ANSWERS

1, Haiphong 2, Isuzu 3, Eric Lubbock 4, Richard Nixon 5, A Soviet telecoms satellite 6, Dominican Republic 7, US Marines 8, Brighton 9, The pope 10, Sir Stanley Matthews (who retired) 11, Steel 12, The Soviet Union's 13, West Germany 14, Runnymede 15, The signing of Magna Carta

QUIZ 201
ARTS & ENTERTAINMENT

. . . .

1 Which actor starred in *A Kind of Loving* (1962)?

2 Who wrote the novel of this title?

3 In which play and film was Archie Rice the main character?

4 Who played him on screen?

5 Who composed *Winter Music* (1960)?

6 Which poet wrote *Summoned by Bells*?

7 Which singer appeared in the film *Work Is A Four Letter Word*?

8 Who directed the movie *Point Blank*?

9 Who wrote a novel called *Stepping Westward*?

10 Who wrote *Forty Years On*?

11 Which actor played a valet in *The Servant*?

12 Who appeared in Seance on a *Wet Afternoon*?

13 What kind of criminal did he play?

14 Which children's illustrator died in 1964?

15 This pianist went to live in Australia in the 60s after success in Britain. Name?

. . . .

ANSWERS

1, Alan Bates 2, Stan Barstow 3, *The Entertainer* 4, Laurence Olivier 5, Richard Rodney Bennett 6, John Betjeman 7, Cilla Black 8, John Boorman 9, Malcolm Bradbury 10, Alan Bennett 11, Dirk Bogarde 12, Richard Attenborough 13, A kidnapper 14, Mabel Lucie Atwell 15, Winifred Atwell

SPORT
1966

• •

1 What nationality was the linesman who gave England's third goal in the 166 World Cup final?

2 For whom had Alf Ramsey played soccer as a professional?

3 Which tennis player was awarded Spain's highest honour in 1966?

4 Which two American football leagues agreed to stage a Superbowl?

5 Who wore the number 9 shirt in England's World Cup winning team?

6 Who said "They think it's all over … it is now"?

7 Who won the 1966 Grand Prix championship in his own car?

8 From which Caribbean island did Gary Sobers come?

9 Who won the first world singles title in bowls in 1966?

10 Who in 1966 began his Test career for West Indies against India with 82?

11 For which English county did he later play?

12 What new rule changed Rugby League in 1966?

13 For which sport was a new Northern League formed, to rejuvenate the game in Britain?

14 Which world title did Age Hadler of Norway win in 1966?

15 Which title did Al Geiberger win?

• •

ANSWERS

1, Russian 2, Southampton and Spurs 3, Manuel Santana 4, National Football League and American Football League 5, Bobby Charlton 6, TV commentator Kenneth Wolstenholme as the 1966 World Cup final ended 7, Jack Brabham 8, Barbados 9, David Bryant 10, Clive Lloyd 11, Lancashire 12, The fourth-tackle rule 13, Ice hockey 14, Orienteering 15, US PGA title

QUIZ 203
PEOPLE

• •

1 Which dancer directed the film *Hello Dolly* in 1969?

2 Where did Chiang Kai-shek rule?

3 How old was Francis Chichester in 1967?

4 What amazing feat had he accomplished on his own?

5 Which Irish statesman was enjoying retirement after being president?

6 The author of *Out of Africa* died in 1962; who was she?

7 In what artform was Placido Domingo building a career?

8 What nationality was he?

9 Who was James Fulbright?

10 With which architectural structure was Buckminster Fuller associated?

11 Of which country was La Bahadur Shastri leader?

12 Which writer created Perry Mason?

13 Which actor starred in the 1964 film *The Best Man*?

14 What were the names of his son and daughter?

15 What kind of show was the daughter taking around US military bases in the mid 60s?

• •

ANSWERS

1, Gene Kelly 2, Taiwan 3, 65 4, Sailed round the world 5, Eamonn de Valera 6, Isak Dinesen 7, Singing (opera) 8, Spanish 9, A US Senator 10, The geodesic dome 11, India 12, Erle Stanley Gardner 13, Henry Fonda 14, Peter and Jane 15, An anti-Vietnam war show

QUIZ 204
ARTS & ENTERTAINMENT

. . . .

1   Which theatre in Stoke on Trent was co-founded by Alan Ayckbourne?

2   To which Yorkshire town did he return in 1964?

3   What was Ayckbourne's first big London hit?

4   Who created the 1962 musical *Blitz!*?

5   What was the name of his 1965 Robin Hood show?

6   How did it fare?

7   Who directed *The Hollow Crown* plays at the Royal Shapespeare Company?

8   Who wrote a "James Bond" novel in 1968?

9   Title?

10   The author of *The Constant Nymph* died in 1967. Who was she?

11   Whose real name is Julie Elizabeth Webb?

12   In which Arthurian role did she star on Broadway in 1960?

13   Which ballet dancer was knighted in 1962?

14   Which dramatist wrote *Ironhand* (1963)?

15   Who presented *Zoo Quest* on television?

. . . .

ANSWERS

PEOPLE

. . . .

1 Which Italian director made the 1960 film *Two Women*?

2 Which US racing drivers won the 1967 Le Mans 24 Hour race?

3 Who made an album called *Lady Soul*?

4 Whose life story (1960) was entitled *My Wicked, Wicked Ways*?

5 Which French leader resigned in 1969?

6 Which painter designed a ceiling for the Paris Opera in 1964?

7 Chester Carlson died in 1968; what piece of office equipment had he invented?

8 Which US cartoonist created "Dogpatch"?

9 Who wrote In *Cold Blood* (1965)?

10 What was it about?

11 Which broadcaster took over Jack Paar's spot on the *Tonight* show on NBC in 1962?

12 Of which country was Papa Doc Duvalier ruler?

13 Which US comedian was known as "Schnozzle"?

14 Which young attorney, later to figure in the Watergate scandal, began working for Richard Nixon?

15 In which sport was Don Carter a US celebrity?

. . . .

ANSWERS

1, Vittorio de Sica 2, Dan Gurney and A J Foyt 4, Errol Flynn 3, Aretha Franklin 5, General de Gaulle 6, Marc Chagall 7, The photocopier 8, Al Capp 9, Truman Capote 10, Real-life murder 11, Johnny Carson 12, Haiti 13, Jimmy Durante 14, John Erlichman 15, Ten pin bowling

QUIZ 206
SPORT
1967

. . . .

1 Where was the first Superbowl staged in 1967?

2 Who won?

3 Who was their head coach?

4 Which team knocked Rangers out of the Scottish Cup in the first round?

5 Whom did Ali beat in February 1967?

6 Why was this a grudge fight?

7 Which teams contested an all-London FA Cup final in 1967?

8 Who won?

9 Who won his first British Open squash title?

10 Who signed Howard Kendall from Preston?

11 Which scrum half made his debut for Wales in Paris?

12 From whom did Liverpool sign Emlyn Hughes?

13 Which goalkeeper also joined Liverpool in 1967?

14 From which club?

15 Who took seven wickets in his first bowl for South Africa?

. . . .

ANSWERS

1, Los Angeles 2, The Green Bay Packers 3, Vince Lombardi 4, Berwick Rangers 5, Ernie Terrell 6, Both claimed to be world champions and Terrell refused to recognize Ali's new name 7, Spurs and Chelsea 8, Spurs 2-1, 9, Jonah Barrington 10, Everton 11, Gareth Edwards 12, Blackpool 13, Ray Clemence 14, Scunthorpe 15, Mike Procter

QUIZ 207
PEOPLE

....

1 Who was the central character in the show *Man from la Mancha*?

2 Which army did General Giap lead?

3 Which French director made a 1968 film called *Weekend*?

4 What kind of band did Kenny Ball lead?

5 With which "sound" was Berry Gordy Jr associated?

6 What instrument did Glenn Gould play?

7 And what nationality was he?

8 Which future Australian prime minister was working for the trade union movement in the 60s?

9 Which actor wrote *Stage Directions* in 1963?

10 What was startling about Rudi Gernreich's 60s bathing suits?

11 Which future British MP played a madwoman in a 1966 film?

12 What was the film?

13 Which future superstar was singing *I Want You Back* with his brothers in 1969?

14 Which sports star was known as "The Golden Jet"?

15 For which North American team did he star?

....

ANSWERS

1. Don Quixote 2. North Vietnam's 3. Jean Luc Godard 4. Trad Jazz band 5. Tamla Motown 6. Piano 7. Canadian 8. Bob Hawke 9. John Gielgud 10. They were topless 11. Glenda Jackson 12. *Marat/Sade* 13. Michael Jackson (with The Jackson Five) 14. Bobby Hull, ice hockey player 15. Chicago Black Hawks

WORLD EVENTS
1965

• •

1 Which party swept to victory in elections in Southern Rhodesia?

2 Why did people on Skye protest at the sight of a ferry?

3 Where did Colonel Boumedienne seize power?

4 Where was Air Marshal Nguyen Cao Ky premier?

5 With whom did Japan establish diplomatic ties in June 1965?

6 Whose MBEs caused protests in some quarters?

7 Who proposed a Commonwealth mission to end the war in Vietnam?

8 What got Gerald Brooke into trouble in Moscow?

9 Who came second in the 1965 Conservative leadership ballot?

10 Who won?

11 Why was this election a Tory first?

12 What was unusual about Heath, educationally, for someone in his position?

13 Which Californian city was hit by riots in 1965?

14 Which district was worst hit?

15 Who declared he would run for the French presidency?

• •

ANSWERS

1, Ian Smith's Rhodesia Front 2, It was the first Sunday ferry service 3, Algeria 4, South Vietnam 5, South Korea 6, The Beatles' 7, Harold Wilson 8, Smuggling "anti-Russian" literature 9, Reginald Maudling 10, Edward Heath 11, It was the first leadership vote by MPs 12, He was the first grammar school boy to lead the Tories 13, Los Angeles 14, Watts 15, Francois Mitterand

QUIZ 209
PEOPLE

. . . .

1 Who was Vice President to Lyndon Johnson?

2 Against whom did he run, and lose, in 1968?

3 This wide-eyed Hungarian-born actor died in 1964. Who was he?

4 What did Courréges design a) cars b) teacups or c) clothes?

5 What was Margaret Court's single name?

6 Which hippy poet organized a "be-in" in San Francisco?

7 Who wrote about "the living sea" in 1963?

8 Which device had this person helped to invent in the 1940s?

9 Who had given up being on the road with Hope?

10 Which crime writer created Gideon of Scotland Yard?

11 With which drinks company was actress Joan Crawford connected?

12 Which famous actress was the mother of Edward Gordon Craig, who died in 1966?

13 Whom did Jacques Couve de Murville succeed?

14 With which branch of US life was George Meany connected?

15 What kind of music did Thelonious Monk play?

. . . .

ANSWERS

1, Hubert Humphrey 2, Richard Nixon 3, Peter Lorre 4, c) Clothes 5, Smith 6, Allen Ginsberg 7, Jacques Cousteau 8, The aqualung 9, Bing Crosby 10, John Creasey 11, Pepsi-Cola (she was a director) 12, Ellen Terry 13, Georges Pompidou 14, Trade unions 15, Jazz

QUIZ 210
PEOPLE

. . . .

1 Who was Liza Minelli's mother?

2 With which movement was James Meredith linked?

3 Which Greek actress starred in the film *Never on Sunday*?

4 What did Zubin Mehta do?

5 Where was he born?

6 Lise Meitner, who died in 1968, was famous as a …?

7 Which Belgian painter died in 1967?

8 Which former Soviet premier was thrown out of the Communist Party in 1961?

9 With which art form was Leonide Massine involved?

10 Which singer appeared with Big Brother and the Holding Co.?

11 Which country did Enver Hoxha lead?

12 For what was Lucky Luciano (died 1962) notorious?

13 Which was Lerner and Loewe's most famous show?

14 Which future Olympic track star was born in the USA in 1961?

15 Which actor won praise for his performance in *The Days of Wine and Roses* (1962)?

. . . .

ANSWERS

QUIZ 211
ARTS & ENTERTAINMENT

· ·

1 Whose last symphony (no. 32) appeared in 1968?

2 Who directed the film *Lord of the Flies*?

3 Who wrote the original book?

4 Which writer seldom left his home in Stromness, Orkney?

5 Who played the mastermind in the film *The League of Gentlemen*?

6 Who played an MP in *No Love For Johnnie*?

7 Which jailed Irish wit and writer did he also play in a film?

8 Who co-starred with Cliff Richard in *Wonderful Life*?

9 Who played the spy who came in from the cold?

10 What was the spy's name?

11 Complete this 1965 film title: *Those Magnificent Men* …

12 Who was Henry VIII in *A Man For All Seasons*?

13 And who played Henry II in *Becket*?

14 Which TV stars played *The Intelligence Men* on the big screen?

15 Who was Juliet in the 1968 film of Shakespeare's tragic love story?

· ·

ANSWERS

1, Havergal Brian 2, Peter Brook 3, William Golding 4, George Mackay Brown 5, Jack Hawkins 6, Peter Finch 7, Oscar Wilde 8, Susan Hampshire 9, Richard Burton 10, Alec Lemass 11, *In Their Flying Machines* 12, Robert Shaw 13, Peter O'Toole 14, Morecambe and Wise 15, Olivia Hussey

QUIZ 212
POT LUCK

. . . .

1 Who starred in *Whack-O!*?

2 Where was this TV show set?

3 For what was Kaffe Fassett winning a name from 1965?

4 Which actor starred as Luther on stage in 1961?

5 Whose real name was William Mitchell, born in London (and not Australia, as many might think)?

6 Whose assistant was Lady Falkender?

7 Who wrote *Jerusalem The Golden* (1967)?

8 In which artform was Antony Dowell a star?

9 Was Colin Davies making his mark as a) an athlete b) an orchestral conductor or c) a singer?

10 Whose autobiography was called *Our Kate* (1969)?

11 Who wrote the stage farce *Chase Me Comrade*?

12 Who was the BBC's chief commentator for all 60s athletic finals?

13 In which musical did Phil Collins appear in 1964?

14 Which British nuclear scientist died in 1967?

15 Top sprinter of the 90s, born 1960 in Jamaica; who was he?

. . . .

ANSWERS

PEOPLE

. . . .

1 Who sang *Fever*?

2 What got Timothy Leary into the news?

3 Which screen heart-throb's real name was Roy Scherer Jr?

4 With which singer-actress did he star in several romantic comedies?

5 Who wrote *Cat and Mouse* (1963)?

6 How long did he have to wait to win the Nobel Prize for literature?

7 What did Hans Kung study and write about?

8 Who was B B King?

9 What fast food chain had Ray Kroc founded and now saw expand?

10 Whose recording of *Ev'ry Time We Say Goodbye* was a family favourite?

11 Who was the subject of Sheridan Morley's biography *A Talent to Amuse*?

12 Was Robert Merrill an opera singer or a dancer?

13 What nationality was novelist Alberto Moravia?

14 Which famous racing driver retired in 1962 after a crash?

15 In what sport has his sister achieved success?

. . . .

ANSWERS

1, Peggy Lee 2, His praise of LSD as a mind-expanding drug 3, Rock Hudson 4, Doris Day 5, Günter Grass 6, Until 1999 7, He was a theologian 8, A musician, known for his guitar playing 9, McDonald's 10, Ella Fitzgerald 11, Noel Coward 12, An American opera singer 13, Italian 14, Stirling Moss 15, Showjumping (Pat Moss)

QUIZ 214
ARTS & ENTERTAINMENT

· ·

1   Which play by Marlowe did Richard Burton film in 1967?
2   Who were the two stars of *Far From The Madding Crowd*?
3   Which film company made *The Devil Rides Out* (1968)?
4   From whose book was this film made?
5   In which studios was the film *2001 – A Space Odyssey* made?
6   Who played the Kaiser in *Oh! What A Lovely War*?
7   And who played Haig?
8   On whose theatre show was this film based?
9   Which comic actor starred in *The Millionairess*?
10 Who was his co-star?
11 Who became famous for saying "I'll give it five" on a TV pop show?
12 In which TV show did Ken Barlow marry Valerie Tatlock?
13 What kind of animal was Mr Ed?
14 Who was Mr Magoo's voice?
15 What was ITV's most successful hospital series?

· ·

ANSWERS

1. *Dr Faustus* 2. Alan Bates and Julie Christie 3. Hammer 4. Dennis Wheatley
5. Elstree 6. Kenneth More 7. John Mills 8. Joan Littlewood's 9. Peter Sellers
10. Sophia Loren 11. Janice Nicholls 12. *Coronation Street* 13. A talking horse
14. Jim Backus 15. *Emergency – Ward 10*

QUIZ 215
POT LUCK

. . . .

1 What did Barry Tuckwell play?

2 What nationality was he?

3 Which instrument did Jack Brymer play?

4 What did Ken Tynan write about?

5 What did Vicky do?

6 Where was he born?

7 His real name?

8 Which British comic was recognized by his skinny legs, long hair, and mad music?

9 In whose serious plays did he sometimes appear?

10 Whose first novel was called *The Fat Woman's Joke*?

11 Which show sparked the first use of the f-word on British television?

12 By what name was William Ambrose Wright better known?

13 To whom was he married?

14 Who was …?

15 What was Norman Wisdom's only US film (1968)?

. . . .

ANSWERS

1. The French horn 2. Australian 3. Clarinet 4. Plays: he was a drama critic 5. He was a cartoonist 6. Germany 7. Victor Weisz 8. Max Wall 9. Samuel Beckett's 10. Fay Weldon's 11. *Oh Calcutta!* 12. Billy Wright, the footballer and for a time TV personality 13. Joy Beverley 14. One of the three singing Beverley sisters 15. *The Night They Raided Minsky's*

WORLD EVENTS
1965

• •

1 Whose ambassador arrived for the first time in Israel?

2 Which ceasefire line did Indian troops cross in August 1965?

3 Where did Chinese celebrate a break with Malays?

4 Whose president was Ayub Khan?

5 What did the US test over the Aleutian Islands in October 1965?

6 Why were eight Moscow soccer players banned for life?

7 Which Indian island state became independent from Britain in 1965?

8 Which UN agency was awarded the 1965 Nobel Peace Prize?

9 What government post did Roy Jenkins assume in December 1965?

10 With which TV programme was Richard Dimbleby most closely associated?

11 Who became President of the Philippines in 1965?

12 What happened to the "Sea Gem" oil rig in the North Sea in 1965?

13 Which writer died at the age of 91 at his home in the south of France?

14 Where did Commonwealth leaders meet in 1966 to discuss Rhodesia?

15 What fate befell Nigeria's government soon afterwards?

• •

ANSWERS

1, West Germany's 2, The Kashmir line 3, Singapore 4, Pakistan's 5, An H-bomb 6, Drunkenness 7, Mauritius 8, UNICEF 9, Home Secretary 10, *Panorama* 11, Ferdinand Marcos 12, It collapsed 13, Somerset Maugham 14, Nigeria 15, It was overthrown by the army

QUIZ 217
PEOPLE

. . . .

1 What game did Paul Newman play in *The Hustler*?

2 Who was his actress wife?

3 In which 1968 film did Newman direct her?

4 What did Dorothea Lange (died 1965) do?

5 What did Liberace have standing on his piano?

6 Which TV actor said good evening beneath a blue lamp?

7 In which organization had Trygve Lie (died 1968) been a key figure?

8 What nationality was he?

9 Who wrote many songs, including *Luck Be a Lady Tonight*, and died in 1969?

10 From which show did this song come?

11 An actor-singer-comedian, his real name was Daniel Kominski; who was he?

12 What instrument did Fritz Kreisler play?

13 Who was regarded as the wealthiest man in the world in the 60s?

14 What nationality was playwright Vaclav Havel?

15 Which American athlete was called "The World's Fastest Human"?

. . . .

ANSWERS

1, Pool 2, Joanne Woodward 3, *Rachel, Rachel* 4, She was a photographer 5, A candelabrum (candle holder) 6, Jack Warner as Dixon of Dock Green 7, The United Nations 8, Norwegian 9, Frank Loesser 10, *Guys and Dolls* 11, Danny Kaye 12, Violin 13, Jean Paul Getty 14, Czech 15, Bob Hayes

QUIZ 218
PEOPLE

. . . .

1 Co-author of *The Front Page*, this writer died in 1964. Name?

2 Who recorded a song called *Hey Joe*?

3 Who created the *Muppets*?

4 On which TV show did they first appear?

5 About what did Hedda Hopper write her columns?

6 What was Gordy Howe's sport?

7 Which Lena was a top 60s singer?

8 Who wrote a controversial play called *Soldiers* in 1967?

9 Why was 1963 a big year for US physicist Richard Feynman?

10 In which country did Dubcek gain and lose power?

11 Whose baby made a 1968 film title?

12 Which Swedish film star was still living as a recluse?

13 What nationality was writer Athol Fugard?

14 Which American dj, involved in the "payola" scandal, died in 1965?

15 What was Milton Friedman's specialist subject?

. . . .

ANSWERS

1, Ben Hecht 2, Jimi Hendrix 3, Jim Henson 4, *Sesame Street* 5, Hollywood and
the stars 6, Ice hockey 7, Lena Horne 8, Rolf Hochhuth 9, He won the Nobel
Prize 10, Czechoslovakia 11, Rosemary's 12, Greta Garbo 13, South African
14, Alan Freed 15, Economics

ARTS & ENTERTAINMENT

1 Who presented *Animal Magic*?

2 Who were Hugh and I?

3 Who starred in *The Marriage Lines*?

4 Who starred in *The Human Jungle*?

5 In which era was the *Sergeant Cork* TV series set?

6 Who played Crane on TV?

7 Where was this series mainly set?

8 Who created a character called Lampwick?

9 What his most popular catchphrase?

10 In which US series did E G Marshall star as a lawyer?

11 Which US comedian had his own show with Mary Tyler Moore as his wife?

12 Which motel opened its doors in Britain in 1964?

13 Who played Meg Richardson in this series?

14 Who were the Clampetts?

15 Who starred as The Virginian?

ANSWERS

1, Johnny Morris 2, Hugh Loyd and Terry Scott 3, Richard Briers and Prunella Scales 4, Herbert Lom 5, Victorian 6, Patrick Allen 7, Morocco 8, Dick Emery 9, Ooh, you are awful ... but I like you 10, *The Defenders* 11, Dick Van Dyke 12, *Crossroads* 13, Noele Gordon 14, The Beverly Hillbillies 15, James Drury

WORLD EVENTS

. . . .

1 What sanctions had Britain imposed to end UDI?

2 Which African state did Sir Albert Margai lead?

3 What had he called on Britain to do about Rhodesia?

4 Who was India's first female prime minister?

5 Which American politician had a wife named Lurleen?

6 What was to be built at Dounreay in Scotland?

7 Where was Aldo Moro prime minister?

8 Which African leader learned he had lost power while in Beijing, China?

9 What was lost from a US plane and then found in Spain?

10 Who announced plans for a cut-price airline in February 1966?

11 Where were Russian writers Sinyavsky and Daniel sent?

12 What was their crime?

13 Who met officially for the first time in 400 years?

14 In which languages did they make speeches?

15 Who was the Anglican leader?

. . . .

ANSWERS

1, Cutting off oil and other trade sanctions 2, Sierra Leone 3, Send troops 4, Indira Gandhi 5, George Wallace 6, A fast-breeder reactor 7, Italy 8, Kwame Nkrumah of Ghana 9, A nuclear weapon 10, Freddie Laker 11, To a labour camp 12, Slandering the Soviet state 13, The heads of the Roman Catholic and Anglican churches 14, Latin and English 15 Archbishop Ramsey

QUIZ 221
PEOPLE

. . . .

1 America's most famous poet died in 1963; who was he?

2 With which medical breakthrough was Howard Florey (died 1968) involved?

3 Which dancer and choreographer directed the 1966 film *Sweet Charity*?

4 ee the poet died in 1962; who was he?

5 What did the Dassault company make?

6 In which country was this company based?

7 And who was its founder?

8 Who announced the setting up of the National Viewers' and Listeners' Association?

9 What year?

10 Which dancer and singer starred in *Oceans 11*?

11 What did Frank Sinatra's friends call themselves?

12 Whose real name was Doris Kappelhof?

13 Complete the title of her last film: *With Six You Get …*?

14 The inventor of the triode died in 1961; who was he?

15 What was the triode used in?

. . . .

ANSWERS

1. Robert Frost 2. The discovery of penicillin 3. Bob Fosse 4. ee cummings (he wrote his name in small letters) 5. Planes and aviation equipment 6. France 7. Marcel Dassault 8. Mary Whitehouse 9. 1965 10. Sammy Davis Jr 11. The Rat Pack 12. Doris Day 13. *Eggroll* 14. Lee De Forest 15. Electronics

QUIZ 222
POT LUCK

1 For which county did Brian Statham play cricket?

2 Where did Harold Macmillan make his "wind of change" speech?

3 What did the initials AMSTRAD stand for in 1968?

4 For which 50s radio show had Eric Sykes written scripts for a wooden dummy?

5 And which comedienne did he partner in a TV comedy series?

6 Was A J P Taylor a) an historian b) a soccer manager or c) a pop singer?

7 Which art gallery had Roy Strong in charge in 1967?

8 Who said that flushing the toilet was the biggest waste of water?

9 Who left Cuba to start revolutions?

10 Which body declared the Jews not guilty of murdering Jesus?

11 Which government resigned in 1965 over television policy?

12 Which company began building DC-9s in Italy?

13 Which army celebrated its 100th birthday in 1965?

14 Who were Jackie Pallo and Mick Macmanus?

15 Which tower became Britain's highest building in 1965?

ANSWERS

1, Lancashire 2, Cape Town 3, Alan M Sugar Trading 4, *Educating Archie* 5, Hattie Jacques 6, a) An historian 7, National Portrait Gallery, London 8, Prince Philip 9, Che Guevara 10, The Vatican 11, The Dutch 12, Douglas 13, The Salvation Army 14, Wrestlers 15, The Post Office Tower in London

QUIZ 223
SCIENCE & TECHNOLOGY

. . . .

1 Was Francis Crick a) British b) Canadian or c) Australian?

2 With which discovery is he associated?

3 Who was his American colleague?

4 Which Nobel prize went to Luis W Alvarez in 1968?

5 In which field?

6 What device used in nuclear research did Donald Glaser of the USA invent?

7 What is cryosurgery: a) using extreme cold b) using extreme heat or c) surgery underwater?

8 What was Enovid 10 (1960)?

9 What form of anti-cancer treatment was first used in 1964?

10 Which chemical added to drinking water aroused controversy?

11 What hovered over lawns in 1963?

12 Which "new" fruit were New Zealanders beginning to market in 1960?

13 By what name was it previously known?

14 Which country first used biodegradable washing powder?

15 When?

. . . .

ANSWERS

1, a) British 2, Genetic code (DNA) 3, James Watson 4, Physics 5, Elementary particle physics 6, The bubble chamber 7, a) Using extreme cold 8, A contraceptive pill 9, Chemotherapy 10, Fluoride 11, The first Flymo lawnmower 12, Kiwi fruit 13, Chinese gooseberry 14, West Germany 15, 1964

PEOPLE

. . . .

1 Which artist called his diary the "diary of a genius"?

2 Which future leader of China lost his job during the Cultural Revolution?

3 Who was the driving force behind this upheaval in China?

4 In which country was Moshe Dayan minister of defence?

5 Who was known as Wilt the Stilt?

6 How many women did he later claim to have slept with?

7 Who starred in the musical *Coco*?

8 Whose story did it it tell?

9 Which goggle-eyed American comedian died in 1964?

10 Which French actress starred in *The Umbrellas of Cherbourg*?

11 Which photographer did she marry in 1965?

12 What first did Elizabeth Lane achieve in British courts in 1965?

13 Which American black activist changed his name to Kwame Touré?

14 What kind of music did A P Carter play?

15 Which future American president was elected to the Georgia state senate in 1963?

. . . .

ANSWERS

1, Salvador Dalí 2, Deng Xiaoping 3, Mao Tse-tung 4, Israel 5, Basketball player Wilt Chamberlain 6, 20,000 7, Katharine Hepburn 8, Coco Chanel's 9, Eddie Cantor 10, Catherine Deneuve 11, David Bailey 12, She was the first woman High Court judge 13, Stokeley Carmichael 14, Country and western 15, Jimmy Carter

QUIZ 225
POT LUCK

. . . .

1 What was "Asterix" doing in space?

2 What did Roger Moore and Patrick McGoohan have in common in 1965?

3 Where did Aleksei Leonov take a walk in 1965?

4 Who was "Goldie" who flew around Regent's Park in London?

5 How did it come to be there?

6 Who designed the new aviary at the zoo (nothing to do with Goldie)?

7 Who married Maureen Cox in 1965?

8 Arthur Stanley Jefferson died in February 1965: who was he?

9 Which of these bands had a number one hit in the USA: a) Steam b) Smoke or c) Gas?

10 And the song title?

11 Who was the first basketball player to score 100 points in a game?

12 For which team?

13 And what year?

14 Which British organization did George Woodcock lead in 1960?

15 Which broadcaster joined RTE in 1963?

. . . .

ANSWERS

1, It was a French satellite launched in 1965 2, They were Britain's highest paid actors 3, In space 4, A golden eagle 5, It escaped from London Zoo 6, Lord Snowdon 7, Ringo Starr 8, Stan Laurel 9, a) Steam 10, Na Na Hey Hey Kiss Him Goodbye 11, Wilt Chamberlain 12, The Philadelphia 76ers 13, 1962 14, The Trades Union Congress 15, Terry Wogan

QUIZ 226
SPORT
1967

. . . .

1 In which sport was Canada's Nancy Greene a champion?

2 Which 100-1 outsider won the 1967 Grand National?

3 What happened at the 23rd fence?

4 Who was the winning jockey?

5 Which animal travelled with the winner, as it usually did on trips?

6 In which stadium was the 1967 League Cup final staged for the first time?

7 Who won?

8 In which division were they then playing?

9 Who played his last US Open in 1967?

10 And who won?

11 In which sport were Malaysians often victorious?

12 Who became the first champion to lose in the first round at Wimbledon?

13 Who beat him?

14 Which German player reached the 1967 Wimbledon men's final?

15 Who beat him?

. . . .

ANSWERS

QUIZ 227
PEOPLE

. . . .

1 Who sang "A Boy Named Sue"?

2 Did Rainer Fassbinder make cars, books or films?

3 What was Jules Feiffer well known for in the USA?

4 He also wrote a play in 1966 – its title?

5 Who wrote *Funeral in Berlin* (1965)?

6 Which of his earlier book titles contained the world "file"?

7 Who starred in the film of this book?

8 Can you remember the name of the character he played?

9 Which impresario presented the Royal Variety Performances?

10 Who was his brother, a big name in British TV?

11 Was Marcel Duchamp a racing driver, a painter or a film star?

12 Whom did Dona Fabiola of Spain marry?

13 In which stadium did the Beatles play in New York in August 1965?

14 How many fans packed in to see them?

15 Which soccer player was knighted in 1965?

. . . .

ANSWERS

1, Johnny Cash 2, Films 3, Cartoons 4, *Little Murders* 5, Len Deighton
6 *The Ipcress File* (1962) 7, Michael Caine 8, Harry Palmer 9, Bernard Delfont
10, Lew Grade 11, A painter 12, King Baudouin of Belgium 13, Shea Stadium
14, 55,000 15, Stanley Matthews

WORLD EVENTS

· ·

1 Which former transport minister lost his shadow cabinet post after the 1966 election?

2 Which country's capital was Kampala?

3 Who married Prince Claes von Amsberg?

4 What had doubled in England and Wales in the period 1956–66?

5 Which country sent its first troops to Vietnam in April 1966?

6 Which airline used its planes to ferry the troops?

7 Who was chosen as the Republican candidate for governor of California in 1966?

8 Where was politician Arthur Calwell wounded in a murder attempt?

9 Who did Irish people refer to as "Dev"?

10 What did the initials UVF stand for in Northern Ireland?

11 What did US aircraft do in Vietnam for the first time in June 1966?

12 Which party did Gwynfor Evans represent in the British Parliament?

13 Who resigned from the British government accusing the prime minister of double-talk?

14 What was the DMZ in Vietnam?

15 Which were the largest bombers used by the Americans in Vietnam?

· ·

ANSWERS

1, Ernest Marples 2, Uganda 3, Princess Beatrix of the Netherlands 4, Illegitimate births 5, Australia 6, Qantas 7, Ronald Reagan 8, Australia 9, Eamon de Valera 10, Ulster Volunteer Force 11, Bombed Hanoi 12, Welsh Nationalists 13, Technology minister Frank Cousins 14, The demilitarized zone between North and South Vietnam 15, B-52s

QUIZ 229
POT LUCK

- -

1 Which theatre did Sheila Van Damm close in 1964?

2 What was her sporting connection?

3 Said to be Britain's greatest sports cartoonist, he died in 1962. Who was he?

4 The inventor of the Dambusters' bouncing bomb was still at work: who was he?

5 What was his "Swallow"?

6 Which British Chancellor of the Exchequer lost his job in the purge of 1963?

7 Which artist created the St Trinian's girls?

8 Where had he been a POW during the war?

9 Which bumbling detective first appeared in a 1963 film?

10 Film title?

11 Who played him?

12 And who played his twitching boss?

13 Which Goon was appearing as a Musketeer in 1967?

14 Who presented TV's *Monitor*?

15 What kind of programme was it?

- -

ANSWERS

1, The Windmill 2, She was a racing driver 3, Tom Webster 4, Sir Barnes Wallis 5, A swing-wing aircraft 6, Selwyn Lloyd 7, Ronald Searle 8, Changi jail, Singapore 9, Clouseau 10, *The Pink Panther* 11, Peter Sellers 12, Herbert Lom 13, Harry Secombe (in *The Four Musketeers*) 14, Huw Wheldon 15, An arts show

PEOPLE
PRESIDENT JOHNSON

. . . .

1 What year did Johnson become vice-president of the United States?

2 What was his full name?

3 In which US state was he born?

4 On which date did he become President?

5 Where was he when the swearing-in ceremony took place?

6 What was Johnson's first order as President?

7 What was his wife's nickname?

8 How many children did the Johnsons have?

9 Their names?

10 Which important law did Johnson sign in July 1964?

11 What year did Johnson win the election to the presidency?

12 Whom did he defeat in that election?

13 Who was his running mate and Vice President?

14 Which name did Johnson coin for his new domestic programme?

15 What historic military commitment did Johnson make during 1965?

. . . .

ANSWERS

1, 1960 2, Lyndon Baines Johnson 3, Texas 4, November 22 1963 5, On board the Presidential jet 6, "Now let's get airborne." 7, Lady Bird 8, Two 9, Lynda Bird and Luci Baines 10, The Civil Rights Bill 11, 1964 12, Barry Goldwater 13, Hubert Humphrey 14, The New Society 15, Sending US troops into South Vietnam

POT LUCK

. . . .

1 Which fictional teacher spoke about her *"crème de la crème"*?

2 What did Julie Felix do?

3 Who directed the 1965 film *Darling*?

4 What did Doug Scott do?

5 The architect of Liverpool's Anglican cathedral died in 1960; his name?

6 What was Ronnie Scott's?

7 What form of transport did Shelia Scott hit the headlines with?

8 Who ran the Slimbridge wildfowl reserve?

9 What was his notable artistic sideline?

10 And whose son was he?

11 Was Cy Grant a runner, a prime minister, or a singer?

12 What did Gerald Scarfe do?

13 Which diplomatic post did Christopher Soames take up in 1968?

14 Who had been his father in law?

15 Which BBC presenter married conductor Georg Solti?

. . . .

ANSWERS

1, Miss Jean Brodie 2, She sang 3, John Schlesinger 4, He climbed mountains 5, Sir Giles Gilbert Scott 6, A jazz club in London 7, She was a long distance aviator 8, Peter Scott 9, He was a painter, especially of birds 10, R F Scott, of the South Pole 11, A singer 12, He was a cartoonist 13, British ambassador to France 14, Winston Churchill 15, Valerie Pitts

PEOPLE

PRESIDENT KENNEDY

• •

1 Who was Kennedy's father?

2 What post had he once held in Britain?

3 In which US state was John Kennedy born?

4 Which university did he attend?

5 In which branch of the military did he serve?

6 Whom did he marry in 1953?

7 Whom did he defeat in the 1960 election for the presidency?

8 How did media coverage of the 1960 campaign differ from all previous elections?

9 What ringing phrase did Kennedy use to describe his programme?

10 How old was Kennedy at his inauguration?

11 Was this significant?

12 In which US city did riots break out in 1961?

13 Which Southern university enrolled its first black student in 1962?

14 Which city saw a Freedom March for civil rights in August 1963?

15 What were the names of the Kennedy children?

• •

ANSWERS

1, Joseph Patrick Kennedy 2, US ambassador 3, Massachusetts 4, Harvard 5, The US Navy 6, Jacqueline Lee Bouvier 7, Richard Nixon 8, The candidates debated face to face on television 9, The New Frontier 10, 43 11, He was the youngest person ever elected 12, Montgomery, Alabama 13, Mississippi 14, Washington DC 15, Caroline and John

QUIZ 233
ARTS & ENTERTAINMENT

1 Who were TV's Bob and Terry?

2 Who played them?

3 Which one of them eventually married Thelma?

4 Who was the first presenter of *Top of the Pops*?

5 What year?

6 Whose first big TV role was as a military policeman in *Redcap*?

7 Was *The Sky at Night* a programme about a) the weather b) the stars or c) bats?

8 Who was its presenter?

9 Which popular British sports show started in 1964?

10 In which TV series did Mia Farrow play Allison Mackenzie?

11 Who played private eye Frank Marker?

12 What was the name of the TV show?

13 What did *Mogul* later become (a new title)?

14 Who wrote the TV play *Vote, Vote, Vote for Nigel Barton*?

15 And who played Nigel Barton?

ANSWERS

1. The Likely Lads 2, Rodney Bewes (Bob) and James Bolam (Terry) 3, Bob 4, Jimmy Savile 5, 1964 6, John Thaw 7, b) The stars 8, Patrick Moore 9, Match of the Day 10, Peyton Place 11, Alfred Burke 12, Public Eye 13, The Troubleshooters 14, Dennis Potter 15, Keith Barron

POT LUCK

· ·

1 Which noted preacher became a life peer in 1965?

2 What (it was said) did the Beatles do in the toilet at Buckingham Palace?

3 Which youthful David joined the Commons in 1965?

4 Which African state became the continent's smallest country in 1965?

5 What did A Wainwright produce until 1966?

6 Who wrote *The Old Men in the Zoo*?

7 At which university did he help run a school of creative writing?

8 With which professor, also a writer?

9 Which Joan starred in many *Carry On* films?

10 And alongside her was the diminutive but busty …?

11 For which magazine was John Wells writing in 1964?

12 Whose spoof diary did he help write?

13 Which playwright wrote *Chips With Everything*?

14 Which actress starred in *Beggar My Neighbour*?

15 She also appeared in *The Spy With the* … what?

· ·

ANSWERS

1, Donald Soper 2, Smoked pot 3, David Steele 4, Gambia 5, Walkers' guides to the Lake District 6, Angus Wilson 7, East Anglia 8, Malcolm Bradbury 9, Joan Sims 10, Barbara Windsor 11, *Private Eye* 12, Mrs Wilson's 13, Arnold Wesker 14, June Whitfield 15, Cold Nose

QUIZ 235

PEOPLE

PRESIDENT KENNEDY

• •

1 Which brother of the President served as Attorney General?

2 Where was the Bay of Pigs?

3 Why did the Bay of Pigs cause Kennedy trouble in 1961?

4 Which Soviet leader did Kennedy confront over a 1962 missile crisis?

5 Where had the offending missiles been installed?

6 Which European crisis city did Kennedy visit?

7 With which British leader did Kennedy apparently get on well, despite the difference in their ages?

8 What was the date of Kenendy's assassination?

9 Which US city was Kennedy visiting at the time of his death?

10 What did superstitious people point to regarding the year of Kennedy's election (1960)?

11 Where was Kennedy going when he was killed?

12 The Governor of Texas was sitting in front of the President, and was wounded when the shooting occurred. Who was he?

13 According to the official version, how many shots were heard?

14 From where were the shots fired?

15 To which hospital in Dallas was President Kennedy taken?

• •

ANSWERS

1. Robert Kennedy 2. Cuba 3. Cuban rebels tried unsuccessfully to invade to overthrow the Communists 4. Khrushchev 5. Cuba 6. Berlin 7. Macmillan 8. November 22 1963 9. Dallas 10. Every US President since William H Harrison (1840) elected in a year ending 0 had died in office 11. To a lunch speech at the Dallas Trade Mart 12. John Connally 13. Three 14. The Texas School Book Depository 15. Parkland Memorial

QUIZ 236
SPORT

. . . .

1 For whom did Engineer play cricket?

2 Who scored a career-best but slow 246 against India for England?

3 In which sport were Hailwood and Agostini rivals?

4 What nationality was golfer Roberto Vicenzo?

5 Which was his big win of 1967?

6 Which British cyclist collapsed and died in 1967 during the Tour de France?

7 Why did New Zealand rugby team refuse to tour South Africa?

8 What was the score in the most one-sided Ryder Cup match ever?

9 Which managerial team arrived at Derby in 1967?

10 Which ex-rider was put in charge of Britain's show jumpers?

11 Which Welsh rugby star switched codes, joining Salford?

12 Which horse became the most expensive ever in Tattersall's December 1967 sales?

13 Why was racing in Britain banned for a month?

14 Which cricketer took seven catches in his first Test match?

15 Which county did he play for?

. . . .

ANSWERS

1, India 2, Geoff Boycott 3, Motor cycle racing 4, Argentinian 5, The Open 6, Tommy Simpson 7, No Maoris were allowed by the apartheid regime 8, 21-6 to the USA 9, Brian Clough and Peter Taylor 10, Pat Smythe 11, David Watkins 12, Vaguely Noble 13, There was an outbreak of foot and mouth disease 14, Alan Knott 15, Kent

QUIZ 237
ARTS & ENTERTAINMENT

1 In which part of Britain was *The Newcomers* set?
2 Which word-spinning panel game began in 1965?
3 Who starred as a copper in *Gideon's Way*?
4 How many people were actually in *The Man In Room 17*?
5 Which detective was played in a series by Douglas Wilmer?
6 Which *Coronation Street* actress got an OBE in 1965?
7 And the character she played?
8 Who was Bertie in *The World of Wooster*?
9 And who was Jeeves?
10 Which organization plotted against the men from UNCLE?
11 Who was the girl from UNCLE?
12 Who starred in *Not Only ... But Also*?
13 Which actress's father voiced *The Magic Roundabout*?
14 What was Brian in this children's show?
15 And Dylan?

ANSWERS

1, East Anglia 2, *Call My Bluff* 3, John Gregson 4, Two 5, Sherlock Holmes 6, Violet Carson 7, Ena Sharples 8, Ian Carmichael 9, Dennis Price 10, THRUSH 11, Stefanie Powers 12, Peter Cook and Dudley Moore 13, Emma Thompson's father Eric 14, A snail 15, A rabbit

PEOPLE

PRESIDENT KENNEDY

. . . .

1 Who was later said to have shot a Dallas policeman while resisting arrest?

2 What was the policeman's name?

3 Who was arrested and charged with the Kennedy murder?

4 In which branch of the US services had the murder suspect served?

5 What was his wife's name?

6 Where had she been born?

7 What happened to the murder suspect on November 24?

8 Who shot him?

9 What day was President Kennedy's funeral?

10 Who represented Queen Elizabeth II at the funeral?

11 Where was the President buried?

12 Which space centre was renamed in his honour?

13 Who led the Commission set up to investigate the killing?

14 What verdict did it deliver in 1964?

15 On which historic site in Britain was a Kennedy memorial built?

. . . .

ANSWERS

15. Runnymede
Canaveral 13. Chief Justice Earl Warren 14. That the killer (Oswald) acted alone
9. Nov 25 10. The Duke of Edinburgh 11. Arlington National Cemetery 12. Cape
5. Marina 6. The USSR 7. He was shot while leaving Dallas city jail 8. Jack Ruby
1. Lee Harvey Oswald 2. J D Tippit 3. Lee Harvey Oswald 4. The Marines

POT LUCK

· ·

1 Which MP called for an inquiry into the cost of contraceptives?
2 What school had new Liberal leader Jeremy Thorpe attended?
3 Which famous American nuiclear scientist died in 1967?
4 For what were Golden Globes awarded?
5 Which US car firm took over Rootes in the UK?
6 Whose show was the most popular BBC offering at Chrstimas 1966?
7 The BOP closed in 1967; what was the BOP?
8 Which detective had featured in its most popular serial?
9 Where were the new Queen Elizabeth Hall and Purcell Room?
10 How many Oscars did *A Man For All Seasons* win in 1967?
11 Who was Britain's first Ombudsman?
12 What was said to have caused the "Apollo 1" spacecraft disaster?
13 How old was Konrad Adenauer at his death in 1967?
14 In which cathedral was his funeral held?
15 What nationality was composer Zoltan Kodaly, who died in 1967?

· ·

ANSWERS

1, Leo Abse 2, Eton 3, Robert Oppenheimer 4, Films 5, Chrysler 6, *The Ken Dodd Show* 7, *The Boys' Own Paper* 8, Sexton Blake 9, The South Bank (Festival Hall) 10, Six 11, Sir Edmund Compton 12, Faulty wiring 13, 91 14, Cologne 15, Hungarian

QUIZ 240
WORLD EVENTS

. . . .

1 Who was the American commander in Vietnam from 1964 to 1968?

2 What was the Ho Chi Minh Trail?

3 What did the name Viet Cong mean?

4 Who were known as hawks and doves?

5 Which US jet fighter suffered a series of crashes in West Germany?

6 Who became South Africa's new prime minister in September 1966?

7 Whom did he succeed?

8 What happened to Dr Verwoerd?

9 How?

10 Which aircraft stole the show at the 1966 Farnborough Air Show by hovering?

11 What kind of vessel was the new "HMS Resolution"?

12 What was happening to Egypt's Abu Simbel temples?

13 Why?

14 Which organization moved its HQ from Paris to Brussels in 1966?

15 Why?

. . . .

ANSWERS

1. General William C Westmoreland 2. A supply route used by the Viet Cong 3. Vietnamese Communists 4. Supporters and opponents of a tougher US military policy in Vietnam 5. The Starfighter 6. Balthasar Vorster 7. Dr Hendrik Verwoerd 8. He was assassinated 9. He was stabbed in Parliament by a messenger 10. The Harrier 11. A nuclear submarine 12. They were being moved 13. To avoid Aswan Dam 14. NATO 15. France had pulled out of NATO

QUIZ 241
ARTS & ENTERTAINMENT

1 Who directed *Cathy Come Home*?

2 And who played Cathy?

3 What kind of creatures were Pinky and Perky?

4 Which knockabout game show began its run in 1966?

5 What kind of animal was Daktari's Clarence?

6 Who starred with Sid James in *George and the Dragon*?

7 Who was The Informer?

8 Who played Adam Adamant?

9 And what was unusual about this crime-fighter?

10 Which actress starred in *The Big Valley*?

11 Who played Batman in the TV series?

12 What did Pan's People do?

13 In the *Forsyte Saga* who played Jolyon Forsyte?

14 Who played Fleur?

15 And who played Irene?

ANSWERS

1. Ken Loach 2. Carol White 3. Puppet pigs 4. *It's A Knockout* 5. A cross-eyed lion 6. Peggy Mount 7. Ian Hendry 8. Gerald Harper 9. He was a 19th-century Victorian, brought back to life in the 1960s 10. Barbara Stanwyck 11. Adam West 12. They were dancers 13. Kenneth More 14. Susan Hampshire 15. Nyree Dawn Porter

QUIZ 242
POT LUCK

. . . .

1 Which boxer lost his crown for refusing to serve?

2 Who won the Eurovision Song Contest in bare feet?

3 What was the song?

4 In which British city was a new Catholic cathedral consecrated?

5 What was stolen from a security van in London in May 1967?

6 Which group released a song called *Itchycoo Park*?

7 Whose records did KNOW radio station in Denver ban?

8 Who suggested the Beatles wear collarless suits?

9 Whose album *Alice's Restautant* was released in 1967?

10 Who was lead singer with The Doors?

11 Which rock 'n' roll magazine made its first appearance in the US in 1967?

12 What was Zilch?

13 Who sang *To Sir With Love* in 1967?

14 Which TV pop show was shown for the last time on 23 December 1966?

15 Which tests for drivers became law in the UK in 1967?

. . . .

ANSWERS

1, Muhammad Ali in 1967 2, Sandie Shaw 3, *Puppet On A String* 4, Liverpool 5, Gold bars worth £700,000 6, The Small Faces 7, The Beatles' 8, Brian Epstein 9, Arlo Guthrie 10, Jim Morrison 11, *Rolling Stone* 12 A boutique in New York City 13, Lulu 14, *Ready Steady Go!* 15, Breath tests

PEOPLE

HAROLD WILSON

• •

1 What were Wilson's full names?

2 Where was he born?

3 What year did he become Britain's prime minister?

4 When had he become an MP?

5 Which constituency had he represented since 1950?

6 When did he first challenge for leadership of the Labour Party?

7 Whom did he eventually replace as leader in 1963?

8 How big was Wilson's majority in the Commons after the 1964 election win?

9 What year did he win a second election, to increase his majority?

10 Was Wilson known as a pipe smoker, a cigar smoker or a cigarette smoker?

11 Which European organization did Britain try and fail to join during the Wilson years?

12 Which African colony proved a thorn in Wilson's side?

13 What was Wilson's wife's name?

14 Which Wilson family pet often featured in press photos?

15 Which was Wilson's favourite holiday destination?

• •

ANSWERS

1, James Harold 2, Huddersfield in Yorkshire 3, 1964 4, 1945 5, Huyton 6, 1960 7, Hugh Gaitskell 8, Five 9, 1966 10, A pipe smoker 11, The Common Market 12, Rhodesia 13, Mary 14, The golden labrador Paddy 15, The Scilly Isles

WORLD EVENTS

• •

1 Of which country was Garfield Todd ex-premier?

2 Of which organization was Lord Robens chairman?

3 Of which organization was J Edgar Hoover boss?

4 Which islands did 22 Argentinians invade in 1966?

5 What were Katyushas?

6 Who used them against an Asian city?

7 Of which country did Jack Lynch become prime minister in 1966?

8 Who met on board HMS "Tiger"?

9 What was the outcome?

10 Whose premier was Borg Olivier?

11 What did he want Britain to do?

12 What was the name of Britain's newest planned city?

13 Where were Red Guards carrying little red books?

14 What did the books contain?

15 What happened to schools in China at this time?

• •

ANSWERS

1, Southern Rhodesia 2, The National Coal Board 3, The FBI 4, The Falklands 5, Russian rockets (dating from World War II) 6, The Viet Cong fired them into Saigon 7, The Irish Republic 8, Harold Wilson and Ian Smith 9, Nothing – the Rhodesians rejected the Wilson proposals 10, Malta's 11, Leave the island 12, Milton Keynes 13, China 14, The thoughts of Chairman Mao Tse-tung 15, Most were closed

QUIZ 245
SPORT

- -

1 Which racing driver was killed at Hockenheim in April 1968?

2 Who said "Winning isn't everything – it's the only thing"?

3 Who won the WBA version of the world heavyweight title in April 1968?

4 Who held the New York version?

5 For which English soccer team did Mick Jones and Terry Cooper play?

6 In which sport did Guy Camberabero excel?

7 Why were three East German sledders disqualified at the 1969 Winter Olympics?

8 What was banned on ski clothing?

9 Which was the first major "open" tennis championship?

10 Whom did Laver beat in the 1968 Wimbledon men's singles final?

11 Who kept goal for Manchester United in their 1968 European Cup final?

12 Who were their opponents?

13 And where was the final played?

14 Who scored United's first goal?

15 What was the final score?

- -

ANSWERS

PEOPLE

. . . .

1 Who wrote an opera called *King Priam*?

2 Who was Felix Topolski?

3 What was Fred Trueman's middle name?

4 Whom did BBC radio listeners vote "man of the decade"?

5 Did Stephen Spender sing, write poems, or ride horses?

6 Where was Sir Georg Solti working in 1961?

7 Which Goon appeared in the film of *Lolita*?

8 Which traveller went in the steps of Marco Polo in 1964?

9 Who was the brunette in the Profumo affair?

10 Which scholar wrote a book called A Cornishman at Oxford?

11 What was Jimmy Savile's first job?

12 Who ran the fraudulent Fire, Auto and Marine insurance scheme?

13 Which brothers opened the Gavroche restaurant in 1967?

14 Which royal went to Benenden School in 1963?

15 Who starred as Sophie Weston in the film *Tom Jones*?

. . . .

ANSWERS

1, Michael Tippett 2, An artist and theatrical designer 3, Harold Wilson 5, He was a poet 6, The Royal Opera House, Covent Garden 7, Peter Sellers 8, Tim Severin 9, Christine Keeler 10, A L Rowse 11, He was a miner 12, Emil Savundra 13, The Roux brothers (Albert and Michel) 14, Princess Anne 15, Susannah York

ARTS & ENTERTAINMENT

. . . .

1 Who was Mrs Thursday?

2 And how had she struck lucky?

3 Which Danger Man star created *The Prisoner*?

4 What "number" was he?

5 How many episodes were there of this cult series?

6 And why was there controversy about the ending?

7 Who played the man in a suitcase?

8 What was he?

9 Who starred as Callan?

10 Who was the first presenter of *The Golden Shot* on British TV?

11 Was he a) American b) Scottish or c) Canadian?

12 Who later took over as the show's host?

13 Which was the most famous cat in British TV commercials?

14 What did he do?

15 Who was the blonde girl co-star of *At Last the 1948 Show*?

. . . .

ANSWERS

1, Katheen Harrison 2, She was a cleaner who inherited £10 million 3, Patrick McGoohan 4, Number Six 5, 17 6, Few people understood it, or were even sure it had ended 7, Richard Bradford 8, A bounty hunter 9, Edward Woodward 10, Jackie Rae 11, c) Canadian 12, Bob Monkhouse 13, Arthur the Kattomeat cat 14, He ate off his paw 15, Aimi Macdonald

POT LUCK

• •

1 Which Duke opened his grounds to flower children?

2 Timothy Leary told youngsters to "turn on, tune in" and … what?

3 Where were 17 former pirate ship djs going to work in 1967?

4 According to a 1965 poll, what did 94 per cent of Britons believe in?

5 Which car company introduced its new Rapier?

6 Who was crowned in Teheran?

7 Whose death was reported from Bolivia?

8 Who was Pu Yi, who also died in 1967?

9 Where did young women with bare breasts taunt police?

10 What dIsaster took place at Hither Green in London?

11 What were to be set up by the new British Countryside Bill?

12 Where did Trevor take over from Peter in 1968?

13 How did this crime-busting slogan end:" Watch out …"?

14 Who set up an Apple shop in London?

15 What did cricketer Fred Titmus lose in a boating accident?

• •

ANSWERS

1, The Duke of Bedford 2, drop out 3, The BBC 4, God 5, Sunbeam 6, The Shah 7, Che Guevara 8, The last emperor of China 9, Anti-war rally in Washington 10, A rail crash 11, Country Parks 12, At Britain's Royal Shakespeare Company 13, There's a thief about 14, The Beatles 15, Four toes

WORLD EVENTS

● ●

1 Which 60s leader had said "a revolution is not a dinner party"?

2 Which Chinese city was the base for oppostion to his cultural revolution?

3 Which killer, seen by millions on TV, died in January 1967?

4 Where was Anastasio Somoza elected president?

5 What vehicles did British police try for the first time?

6 Whose daughter defected from Russia to the West?

7 What was her name?

8 Whose appointment caused turmoil at the LSE?

9 Why?

10 What was described as "the greatest peacetime threat to Britain"?

11 Where did Army generals seize power in Europe in 1967?

12 Who called Britain "the sick man of Europe"?

13 Of which board was Mark Bonham-Carter first chairman?

14 Who called for an end to the Anglo-American special relationship?

15 Where was Yakubu Gowon holding power?

● ●

ANSWERS

1, Mao (in 1927) 2, Shanghai 3, Jack Ruby 4, Nicaragua 5, Helicopters 6, Stalin's 7, Svetlana Alliluyeva 8, Walter Adams 9, He was former head of Rhodesia's University College 10, The Torrey Canyon oil disaster 11, Greece 12, Enoch Powell 13, The Race Relations Board in Britain 14, De Gaulle 15, Nigeria

QUIZ 250
PEOPLE

. . . .

1 Who went to work for Lonrho in 1961?

2 Which Welsh soccer star was born at St Asaph in 1961?

3 What instrument did Semprini play?

4 Where was he born: a) Paris b) Rome c) Bath?

5 What nationality was Lynn Seymour?

6 And what did she do?

7 Who wrote The *Ballad of Peckham Rye*?

8 Who first presented ITV's *World of Sport*?

9 Which philosopher tore up his Labour Party membership card?

10 Why?

11 Who said "I've been on a calendar, but never on time"?

12 Whose initials were RFK?

13 Which artist painted *Christ in Majesty* in Coventry Cathedral?

14 What post did Michael Stewart hold from 1965 to 1966?

15 Who made the funny film *The Plank* in 1967?

. . . .

ANSWERS

1, Tiny Rowlands 2, Ian Rush 3, Piano 4, c) Bath 5, Canadian 6, She was a ballet dancer 7, Muriel Spark 8, Eamonn Andrews 9, Bertrand Russell 10, To protest at Britain's support for the USA in the Vietnam War 11, Marilyn Monroe 12, Robert Fitzgerald Kennedy 13, Graham Sutherland 14, British Foreign Secretary 15, Eric Sykes

QUIZ 251
POT LUCK
1968

• •

1 What was the Galaxy, unveiled in 1968?

2 And what was Rolls Royce's RB-211?

3 What was the first name of Martin Luther King's wife?

4 With which bank did Barclays merge in 1968?

5 Who sailed home to Portsmouth in July 1968?

6 Where had he been?

7 And the yacht's name?

8 Who issued a 1968 document called *Humanae Vitae*?

9 What was its main message?

10 What was the best known flower-child greeting?

11 Which new Underground line was partly opened in 1968?

12 What did banks in Britain announce they would do on Saturdays?

13 How much did a first-class stamp cost in 1968, when two-tier post was introduced?

14 Which literary prize was new in 1969?

15 Which two "overseas" ministries merged?

• •

ANSWERS

QUIZ 252
PEOPLE

. . . .

1 What musical instrument did Oscar Peterson play?

2 Which black actor starred in *Guess Who's Coming To Dinner*?

3 Which veteran actor co-starred with him?

4 He wrote *High Society*, and died in 1964; who was he?

5 Who was Hal Porter?

6 Which British actress starred in Morgan?

7 Who was her actor brother?

8 By what name was Emmanuel Goldenberg known in films?

9 What did Kenny Rogers sing?

10 Which US comic appeared as Uncle Albert in *Mary Poppins*?

11 What year did he die?

12 Who sang *D-I-V-O-R-C-E*?

13 What she did memorably tell girls to do?

14 Which British archaeologist died in 1960?

15 Which Mesopotamian site had he explored?

. . . .

ANSWERS

1, Piano 2, Sidney Poitier 3, Spencer Tracy 4, Cole Porter 5, An Australian writer
6, Vanessa Redgrave 7, Corin 8, Edward G Robinson 9, Country and western
10, Ed Wynn 11, 1966 12, Tammy Wynette 13, Stand By Your Man 14, Sir Leonard
Woollet 15, Ur

QUIZ 253
POT LUCK

. . . .

1 Who presented *Whicker's World* on television?

2 Which Welsh rugby-playing doctor gained his first cap in 1969?

3 What nationality was composer Malcolm Williamson?

4 Complete this opera title by him (1963): *Our Man in …*?

5 What did C F Tunnicliffe paint?

6 Was John Wood an actor, a cricketer, or Victoria Wood's father?

7 Which band featured in the film *Gimme Shelter*?

8 Which action by John Kennedy Jr caught all the cameras during his father's funeral?

9 Which spy case rocked Britain in 1962?

10 Where was Joan Sutherland born: a) Canada b) Britain or c) Australia?

11 What did she do?

12 Whose real name was Tommy Hicks?

13 In which play by Goldsmith did he appear in 1960?

14 Who was Sir William Stanier, who died in 1965?

15 What sport did Fred Titmus play?

. . . .

ANSWERS

QUIZ 254
SCIENCE & TECHNOLOGY

· ·

1 Which car company developed (1966) a sealed water-cooling system?

2 What was the Atlas?

3 What kind of nuclear reactor was at Dounreay?

4 What was the takamak (1963) used to study?

5 Where was the world's first solar thermal power plant (1960)?

6 What did Albert Caquot of France design: a) cars b) tidal power stations or c) hi-tech clothing?

7 Can water jets be used to cut materials?

8 When was this first done?

9 What particles were first called "aces"?

10 What are Up, Down, Strange, Charm, Bottom and Top?

11 What was on top of Mount Palomar?

12 What went up for the first time in 1962 from Russia?

13 What mysterious space phenomena were first named in 1967?

14 What orbited the Earth at 327 km (203 miles) high in 1961?

15 How many manned space stations were in orbit by 1969?

· ·

ANSWERS

QUIZ 255
PEOPLE

1 What language was Arthur Waley expert at translating?

2 What post did Enoch Powell hold from 1960–63?

3 Whose arrival did he say was unwise and likely to cause social unrest?

4 Who was Leontyne Price?

5 Which US poet known for his cantos was living in exile in Italy?

6 What instrument did Itzhak Perlman play?

7 Where was he born?

8 Which Argentine leader went in exile in Spain in 1960?

9 Whose *Tonight* TV show was renamed after him?

10 For which qualities was he renowned?

11 Who was Satchel Paige?

12 How old was he when he played his last game in 1965?

13 Who was Kenny Rogers?

14 Which retired cowboy had a horse called Trigger?

15 Which poet got a knighthood in 1969?

ANSWERS

1. Chinese 2. Minister of Health 3. Commonwealth immigrants to Britain 4. An American opera singer 5. Ezra Pound 6. Violin 7. Israel 8. Juan Peron 9. Jack Paar 10. Irreverence and irritability 11. An American baseball player 12. Probably 59 13. A country and western singer 14. Roy Rogers 15. John Betjeman

PEOPLE

. . . .

1 What was Elvis Presley's middle name?

2 Which soccer player was nicknamed "Chopper"?

3 Which US baseball star was known as "Charlie Hustle"?

4 Who was Lewis Brian Hopkins-Jones?

5 Who was reckoned the 60s finest classical pianist?

6 Whose book was called *I'm Sorry I Kept You Waiting Madam*?

7 Who was the Vaulting Vicar?

8 And who was Lynn the Leap?

9 What did Harold (Hal) Prince produce?

10 Who was Josh White, who died in 1969?

11 Who directed *The Fortune Cookie*?

12 Where was he born?

13 Who led the Tijuana Brass?

14 Whom did the Beatles christen Sexy Sadie?

15 Who collapsed in 1966 after a 20-minute drum solo?

. . . .

ANSWERS

1, Aron 2, Ron Harris of Chelsea 3, Pete Rose 4, Brian Jones of The Rolling Stones 5, Arthur Rubinstein 6, Vidal Sassoon 7, American athlete Bob Richards 8, Welsh long jumper Lynn Davis 9, Stage shows 10, A blues singer 11, Billy Wilder 12, Austria 13, Herb Alpert 14, The Maharishi 15, Ginger Baker of Cream

POT LUCK

. . . .

1 In which ministry did Margaret Thatcher get her first government job (1961)?

2 Which gap-toothed comic sported a cigarette holder?

3 In which country outside Britain did he become a favourite?

4 Who became leader of the Liberal Party in 1967?

5 Whom did he succeed?

6 On what did Ian Trethowan comment for ITV?

7 Which rival organization did he later move to?

8 What did Home, Light and Third become?

9 Which cartoonist drew Flook?

10 Which instrument did Stan Tracey play?

11 Whose catchphrase was "You lucky people"?

12 Of which city was Willy Brandt mayor?

13 Who said "A great nation must move on"?

14 When?

15 What US government post was held by Dean Rusk?

. . . .

ANSWERS

1, Ministry of Pensions and National Insurance 2, Terry-Thomas 3, The United States 4, Jeremy Thorpe 5, Jo Grimond 6, Politics 7, The BBC 8, Radio 1, 2, 3 & 4 9, Trog 10, Piano 11, Tommy Trinder's 12, West Berlin 13, President Johnson 14, In 1963, after the death of President Kennedy 15, Secretary of State

QUIZ 258
POT LUCK

- -

1 What were winklepickers?

2 What were stilettos?

3 What did 60s students do at a hop?

4 What were Park Drive and Woodbines?

5 What would you have done with a duffel?

6 Did teenagers wear trainers?

7 How about jeans?

8 What was often mixed with Baccardi?

9 What was a Dansette?

10 What did older people still call record players?

11 What kind of tape recorders could people use at home in 1960?

12 In what year was Nelson Mandela sentenced to life imprisonment?

13 Who went on the annual Aldermaston march in Britain?

14 Did people cook with microwaves in 1965?

15 What was Smash?

- -

ANSWERS

mashed potato

1, Pointed shoes 2, High, thin heels 3, Dance and drink beer mostly 4, British cigarette brands 5, Worn it (it was a coat) 6, No (they were not fashion items in the 60s) 7, Oh yes 8, Coke 9, A record player 10, Gramophones 11, Reel to reel machines (no cassettes yet) 12, 1964 13, CND supporters 14, No 15, Instant

QUIZ 259
ARTS & ENTERTAINMENT

1 Which news programme first went on air in Britain in 1967?

2 Who were the first presenters?

3 Who starred in *Not In Front Of The Children*?

4 Which Western series starred Leif Erickson?

5 Who presented the *Laugh-In*?

6 Who was the show's dumb blonde?

7 And who was the "sock-it-to-me" girl?

8 What kind of animal was Basil Brush?

9 Who played a foolish friar in *Oh Brother*?

10 What kind of crime expert was *The Expert*?

11 And who played him?

12 What year was *The Royal Family* television documentary?

13 Who presented *Stars on Sunday*?

14 Who played Paul Temple on TV?

15 Who were the three girls in *Take Three Girls*?

ANSWERS

1, *News At Ten* 2, Andrew Gardner and Alastair Burnet 3, Wendy Craig 4, *The High Chaparal* 5, Dan Rowan and Dick Martin 6, Goldie Hawn 7, Judy Carne 8, A fox 9, Derek Nimmo 10, A pathologist 11, Marius Goring 12, 1967 13, Jess Yates 14, Francis Matthews 15, Sudan Jameson, Lisa Goddard and Angela Down

SCIENCE & TECHNOLOGY

1 What was the TU-144?

2 Was the Hunter a) a jet fighter b) a type of submarine or c) a helicopter?

3 What were the Black Arrows?

4 Was the Centurion a) a battleship b) a tank or c) a rocket?

5 Which was the biggest US bomber used in the Vietnam War?

6 What was the SR-71?

7 Which famous Russian warplane made its debut in 1965?

8 What was its NATO codename?

9 How fast could it fly: a) 1500 mph b) 1700 mph or c) 2100 mph?

10 Who met his death in a MiG-15 in 1968?

11 Which anti-submarine aircraft entered RAF service in 1969?

12 From which civil airliner had it been developed?

13 Which US jet fighter entered Royal Navy service in 1968?

14 What was the Walleye?

15 What year did Harriers enter RAF service?

ANSWERS

1, Russia's supersonic airliner, 2, a) A jet fighter 3, The RAF's aerobatic team 4, b) A tank 5, The Boeing B-52 6, A very fast spy plane 7, The MiG-25 8, Foxbat 9, c) 2100 mph 10, Yuri Gagarin 11, Nimrod 12, The Comet 13, The Phantom 14, A guided bomb 15, 1969

POT LUCK

. . . .

1 Did people in Britain have colour TV in 1960?

2 What did the initials LP stand for?

3 What was an EP record?

4 What were styluses?

5 What kind of pens did people use at school?

6 What was blotting paper?

7 How did most people heat their homes?

8 What were popular in cavalry twill?

9 What did Americans mean by sneakers?

10 What were ousting suspenders for girls?

11 What did many working women wear on their heads?

12 And what did many men still wear, and raise when they met a woman they knew?

13 What was the most popular takeaway in Britain?

14 What did people think of when they heard the name Butlins or Pontins?

15 Which part of a girl might have been "bouffant"?

. . . .

ANSWERS

1, No 2, Long playing (as in record) 3, Extended play record (four tracks) 4, A long-life "needle" fixed into the pickup head fo therecord player. 5, Mostly ink pens 6, Absorbent paper used to dry ink writing 7, In Britain, by coal, gas or electric fires. Central heating was common only in the USA 8, Men's trousers 9, Light canvas shoes 10, Tights 11, Scarves 12, Hats 13, Fish and chips 14, Holiday camps 15, Her hair

SPORT

· ·

1 From whom did George Halas retire as head coach in May 1968?

2 From which club did Francis Lee join Manchester City?

3 Who was the first to run 100m in under 10 seconds?

4 For which soccer club did Jeff Astle play?

5 Who won the Scottish Cup for only the second time in their history?

6 Who was the first England player to be sent off in an international?

7 What was his offence?

8 Did England win?

9 Against whom were England playing?

10 Which golfer recorded a record-breaking four below-70 rounds in the US Open?

11 Which country won Rugby League's World Cup?

12 In which sport was the May 11 game christened the "watersplash final"?

13 Who were the two teams?

14 How many Test matches did the British Lions win in South Africa?

15 Who rode Sir Ivor to win the Derby?

· ·

ANSWERS

1, The Chicago Bears football team 2, Bolton Wanderers 3, Jim Hines 4, West Bromwich Albion 5, Dunfermline 6, Alan Mullery 7, Retaliation after a foul 8, No, they lost 1-0 9, Yugoslavia 10, Lee Trevino 11, Australia 12, The Rugby League final 13, Leeds beat Wakefield 11-10 14, None (lost 3, drew 1) 15, Lester Piggott

QUIZ 263
SCIENCE & TECHNOLOGY

. . . .

1 Which US airline was first to fly Boeing 747s?

2 What did SST stand for?

3 What was the standard long-range airliner of the 60s?

4 The US Douglas company had a rival plane; what was it?

5 Which was Britain's only long-range jet airliner, still used by the RAF?

6 What were the names of the RAF's three V bombers?

7 Which had a delta wing?

8 Britain's first supersonic jet fighter entered service in 1960. What was it?

9 By what name was the American F-105 fighter-bomber also known?

10 What was the USAF's first supersonic bomber, in 1960?

11 What was the Snark?

12 What flying first linked Britain and Australia in June 1961?

13 Which US planes scored the first combat victories in Vietnam in 1965?

14 What kind of plane was the Belfast of 1964?

15 Which swing-wing plane first flew in 1964 in Texas?

. . . .

ANSWERS

QUIZ 264
PEOPLE

. . . .

1 Dave Dee went with ... who?

2 What had Dave Dee been before becoming a pop singer?

3 Who sang *Cinderella Rockefella*?

4 Who was Bud Powell?

5 What did Charley Pride sing?

6 Where did Muhammad Reza Pahlevi reign?

7 Who was Samantha Eggar?

8 Which tenor made his debut at La Scala in 1965?

9 Where was Park Chung Hee president in 1963?

10 What did Grote Reber study?

11 Who was Billy Rose?

12 Which cosmetics supremo died in 1965?

13 Where was she born?

14 Who played General Turgidson in *Dr Strangelove*?

15 Who directed the film?

. . . .

ANSWERS

1, Dozy, Beaky, Mick and Tich 2, A policeman 3, Esther and Abi Ofarim 4, An American jazz pianist, who died in 1966 5, Country and western 6, Iran 7, A British actress 8, Pavarotti 9, South Korea 10, The stars (he was a US astronomer) 11, An American showman 12, Helena Rubinstein 13, Poland 14, George C Scott 15, Stanley Kubrick

POT LUCK

1 Could you buy stereo records in 1960?

2 What kind of journalist was "Evelyn Home"?

3 What was wrong with Richard Nixon's appearance on TV in 1960?

4 What were "jingles"?

5 Was the Mini's engine in front or at the back?

6 What did Victor Silvester studios teach?

7 What was their US equivalent?

8 What kind of artist was Roy Liechtenstein?

9 What new card became available in Britain in 1963?

10 What were claimed to be "as cool as a mountain stream"?

11 Which sign meant "happy motoring" according to the ads?

12 "Which twin has the Toni?" was an advert for what?

13 How much would did an Austin 1800 car cost in 1969?

14 What was a Double Two?

15 What did BSR make?

ANSWERS

1, Yes, since 1958 2, She was an agony aunt, editing the letters page in a women's magazine 3, His dark stubble made him look shifty, and he appeared tense 4, Catchy tunes or songs used in TV commercials 5, In the front 6, Dancing 7, Arthur Murray 8, A pop artist 9, American Express 10, Menthol flavour cigarettes 11, The Esso sign 12, Hair perm 13, About £1000 14, A man's shirt 15, Turntables for record players

QUIZ 266
PEOPLE

· ·

1 How many golds did Mark Spitz win at the 1968 Olympics?

2 Were they solo races or relays?

3 What did Kim Stanley do by the method?

4 Where was Cardinal Spellman archbishop?

5 Was Sirhan Sirhan executed for shooting Robert Kennedy?

6 Who was Upton Sinclair, who died in 1968?

7 Which branch of science did Glenn Seaborg pioneer?

8 Who sang *Honey* in 1968?

9 Who was Josef von Sternberg, who died in 1969?

10 With which actress did he famously work pre-war?

11 What nationality was Mikas Theodorakis?

12 Was he a composer, a politician, or a cook?

13 What did Jack Teagarden play?

14 Who was Lord Tedder?

15 In which invasion had he played an important part in World War II?

· ·

ANSWERS

1. Two 2. Relays 3. Act. She was famous for her Method approach 4. New York 5. No, the sentence was commuted to life 6. An American writer 7. Nuclear power 8. Bobby Goldsboro 9. A film director 10. Marlene Dietrich 11. Greek 12. A composer 13. Trombone 14. A British air marshal 15. D-Day

WORLD EVENTS

. . . .

1 Which breakaway state was led by Colonel Ojukwu?

2 Where did this breakaway lead to civil war?

3 Who were the majority people in the breakaway state?

4 What was the UAR?

5 What was Thurgood Marshall the first black member of?

6 Where were 18 Britons shot dead in a police mutiny?

7 What began on 5 June 1967?

8 Which strip did Israel take from Egypt?

9 Which biblical towns did Israel capture from Jordan?

10 At which special site did Israeli troops pray on 7 June?

11 Whose resignation was rejected by mass rallies?

12 Which country lost most of the West Bank in the war?

13 Which ex-king was greeted by his niece in London?

14 Which part of Canada did De Gaulle visit?

15 Who was pulling out "east of Suez"?

. . . .

ANSWERS

ARTS &
ENTERTAINMENT

· ·

1 Whose first US hit was *Last Train to Clarksville*?

2 Which "tabletop" TV show started in 1969?

3 Which comedian starred in *Sez Les*?

4 Who was the star of *Up Pompeii*?

5 In which US show did a man stay on the run until 1967?

6 Who played him?

7 Who played the suave smoothie in *Hadleigh*?

8 What was Ken Dodd's most famous record?

9 Did it top the charts?

10 What were the Stones telling us to "get off" in 1965?

11 Who played bass with the Stones?

12 Who had a 1966 hit with *Morningtown Ride*?

13 Which Lee wrote and recorded with Nancy?

14 *Reach Out I'll Be There* was a hit for which US group?

15 Who sang *All For Nothing* (1966)?

· ·

ANSWERS

1. The Monkees 2. *Pot Black* 3. Les Dawson 4. Frankie Howerd 5. *The Fugitive* 6. David Janssen 7. Gerald Harpe 8. *Happiness* 9. No, it peaked at 34 10. *My Cloud* 11. Bill Wyman 12. The Seekers 13. Lee Hazelwood (with Nancy Sinatra) 14. The Four Tops 15. The Small Faces

QUIZ 269
POT LUCK

. . . .

1 What drink was advertised by the slogan … "Schhh… You-Know-Who"?

2 What were Dizzy Bug and Headache, new in 1969?

3 Which car firm made the Ami 8?

4 What was Three Nuns?

5 Which Lancashire town was hit by a polio epidemic in 1965?

6 Which vaccine was used widely in Britain to fight polio?

7 Where was the Manned Spacecraft Centre?

8 What did Gerald Moore retire from in 1965?

9 What was "Sea Egg" (1965)?

10 Who was in it?

11 Who was Ophelia to David Warner's 1965 Hamlet?

12 Where was Jack Dash an unofficial leader?

13 What did he describe as "a docker's dream" in 1965?

14 Scot Willie Gallacher was buried in 1965; what political persuasion was he?

15 What job did Ray Gunter hold in Britain's Labour government?

. . . .

ANSWERS

WORLD EVENTS
1967

• •

1 What became legal in Britain in 1967?

2 Which US city was hit by riots in July 1967?

3 The riots began in a "blind pig": what was that?

4 Of which province in Canada was Daniel Johnson premier?

5 What happened to George Rockwell in August 1967?

6 Which ex-child star said she would stand for Congress?

7 Whose diplomatic HQ in London was the scene of fighting?

8 What aircraft did Britain, France and West Germany agree to build?

9 Who said the Vietnam War should be stepped up to end it quickly?

10 Which rock's people voted to stay British?

11 Where was Enugu?

12 Who captured it in October 1967?

13 Which country had a new leader in John McEwen?

14 What was Groote Schur?

15 What was rolled out at Toulouse in December 1967?

• •

ANSWERS

1, Abortions 2, Detroit 3, An illegal drinking shop 4, Quebec 5, He was shot dead 6, Shirley Temple Black 7, China's 8, The Airbus 9, Ronald Reagan 10, Gibraltar 11, It was the capital of Biafra 12, Federal Nigerian troops 13, Australia 14, A hospital in South Africa where the first heart transplant was performed 15, The first Concorde

PEOPLE

• •

1 Which New Zealander sang for the first time in London in 1969?

2 Who sang with the Shondells?

3 And with the Pirates?

4 Who was Edward Bond?

5 Which man in the news in 1969 was born in Wapakoneta, Ohio, in 1930?

6 What was his middle name?

7 Of which state did Spiro Agnew become governor in 1966?

8 Which clothes-off show did Michael Butler bring to Broadway?

9 Which ship did Lloyd Bucher command?

10 Who was Angie Brooks?

11 Who was born Herbert Frahm in Lubeck in 1913?

12 Who went to Timbertop school for two months in 1966?

13 Where was this school?

14 What post did Charles Evers win in 1969?

15 Was Abe Fortas an American judge or a South African rugby player?

• •

ANSWERS

1. Kiri Te Kanawa 2. Tommy James 3. Johnny Kidd 4. A British playwright 5. Neil Armstrong 6. Alden 7. Maryland 8. *Hair* 9. The spy ship USS "Pueblo" 10. A UN official, president of the General Assembly in 1969 11. Willy Brandt 12. Prince Charles 13. Victoria, Australia 14. First black mayor of a town in Mississippi called Fayette 15. An American judge

QUIZ 272
POT LUCK

. . . .

1 Which Beatle appeared on his own in the film *How I Won The War*?

2 Who married Aristotle Onassis?

3 Where were England not going to play cricket?

4 What was going to make childbirth less painful?

5 What was British Eagle?

6 For what crime was Bruce Reynolds arrested in November 1968?

7 What was the "Tribal-Love-Rock" musical?

8 What did the cast do on stage?

9 Who wrote *Myra Breckinridge*?

10 And who was the author of *Couples*?

11 Whose novels were smuggled out of Russia to the West?

12 Who said "I've looked and I've seen the promised land"?

13 Which 1969 skirt length dropped hemlines?

14 What kind of fair ran for six days in Copenhagen in 1969?

15 And what had just been abolished in Denmark?

. . . .

ANSWERS

1, John Lennon 2, Jackie Kennedy 3, South Africa (the planned tour was cancelled) 4, The epidural 5, An airline which went bust 6, His part in the Great Train Robbery 7, *Hair* 8, Appear naked (among other things) 9, Gore Vidal 10, John Updike 11, Alexander Solzhenitsyn's 12, Martin Luther King 13, The maxi 14, A sex fair 15, Censorship of pornography

QUIZ 273
SCIENCE & TECHNOLOGY

. . . .

1 What were Elfe and Cirrus, and where might they have travelled?
2 Boeing abandoned the B-2707 in 1968; what was it?
3 Which giant airplane first flew in June 1968?
4 The British government cancelled TSR-2; what was it?
5 What in 1968 did the UK government announce Britain would do, measurement-wise?
6 What name did Hillman give its "Mini"?
7 Which British carmaker produced the Herald?
8 What were Lambrettas?
9 Were seat belts compulsory in the UK by 1969?
10 What kind of vehicle was the Ski-Doo?
11 Where was it invented?
12 What new train was tested at Pueblo, USA, in 1967?
13 Which country introduced the Bullet train?
14 When?
15 Which two cities were linked by Bullet services?

. . . .

ANSWERS

1, In the air, they were sailplanes or gliders 2, A planned supersonic airliner 3, The Lockheed C-5A Galaxy 4, A new strike aircraft for the RAF 5, Go metric 6, The Imp 7, Triumph 8, Scooters 9, No (1983) 10, A snow scooter 11, Canada 12, A maglev 13, Japan 14, 1964 15, Tokyo and Osaka

SPORT

1968

• •

1 Which world record did Bob Beamon obliterate in the 1968 Olympics?

2 And by what distance (in centimetres)

3 Which Olympic athletes wore black gloves and raised their fists on the victory stand?

4 Why?

5 How many gold medals did Britain win?

6 Which Briton won the men's 400-metre hurdles?

7 Which South African batsman made hay playing for Hampshire in 1968?

8 Which country did Wales play an international rugby match against for the first time?

9 Who won?

10 Who was the first black player to win a major men's tennis title?

11 Which title did he win in 1968?

12 Which bowler took six wickets against Australia and was then dropped?

13 Which car was Jackie Stewart driving in the 1968 Grand Prix season?

14 Who were 1968 World Series baseball winners?

15 Who won the cricket county championship for the third year in a row?

• •

ANSWERS

1, The long jump 2, 55 cm 3, Lee Evans and John Carlos of the USA 4, They were supporting Black Power 5, Five 6, David Hemery 7, Barry Richards 8, Argentina 9, Argentina 10, Arthur Ashe 11, The US Open 12, Pat Pocock 13, Matra 14, Detroit Tigers 15, Yorkshire

QUIZ 275
POT LUCK

1 Who became the new Czech ambassador to Turkey in December 1969?

2 Where did the bikers in *Easy Rider* begin their journey?

3 What was the first sport to be shown in colour on British TV?

4 Which star of *Gone With The Wind* died in 1967?

5 In which film did Redford and Fonda play newlyweds?

6 Whom did Henry Cooper beat in 1967 to win his third Lonsdale Belt?

7 What was Alec Rose's job when not sailing?

8 Who sang *Hello Goodbye*?

9 Where was milk no longer free after 1968?

10 In which country did Tony Hancock commit suicide?

11 Which banknote was the 50p piece to replace?

12 Which veteran jazzman sang his way to the top of the charts in May 1968?

13 With which song?

14 How old was he?

15 What nationality was Olympic discus thrower Al Oerter?

ANSWERS

1, Alexander Dubcek 2, Los Angeles 3, Wimbledon tennis 4, Vivien Leigh 5, *Barefoot In The Park* 6, Billy Walker 7, A greengrocer 8, The Beatles 9, British secondary schools 10, Australia 11, The ten shilling note 12, Louis Armstrong 13, *What A Wonderful World* 14, 67 15, American

QUIZ 276
WORLD EVENTS
1968

1 Which baby expert got into trouble for his Vietnam protests?
2 Who attacked the ship "Pueblo"?
3 What was this ship said to be?
4 Where did Alexander Dubcek take power?
5 From which African state did Asian refugees fly to Britain?
6 What kind of plane crashed off Greenland?
7 Where was the Tet offensive?
8 What was Tet?
9 Which city was attacked?
10 Where were 30 US planes reportedly destroyed?
11 Which old imperial city was captured by the Viet Cong, then retaken?
12 Which London square was the scene of violent anti-war protests?
13 Why there?
14 Which actress was prominent in anti-war meetings?
15 Who stunned America by saying he would not run?

ANSWERS

1, Benjamin Spock 2, North Koreans 3, A spy ship 4, Czechoslovakia 5, Kenya 6, An American B-52 7, Vietnam 8, The Vietnamese New Year 9, Saigon 10, Da Nang 11, Hue 12, Grosvenor Square 13, The US Embassy is there 14, Vanessa Redgrave 15, President Johnson

QUIZ 277
ARTS & ENTERTAINMENT

- -

1 Which US singer covered the Stones' *Satisfaction* in 1966?

2 Which group sang *Pretty Flamingo*?

3 Paint It Black was a number one for …?

4 Which group complained "The sun ain't gonna shine anymore"?

5 Who sang *Out of Time*?

6 Who sang *The Ballad of Bonnie and Clyde*?

7 What was The Foundations' biggest hit?

8 Cass Elliott and Michelle Gilliam were two of the …?

9 Who sang *Rainy Day Woman* No.s 12 and 35?

10 Which British singer made way for Engelbert Humperdinck at the London Palladium?

11 Which was the newcomer's first British chart topper?

12 Who won the 1967 Eurovision Song Contest?

13 And the song?

14 Whose silence was golden in 1967?

15 Who had left them the previous year?

- -

ANSWERS

1. Otis Redding 2, Manfred Mann 3, The Rolling Stones 4, The Walker Brothers
5, Chris Farlowe 6, Georgie Fame 7, *Baby Now That I've
Found You* 8, Mamas and Papas 9, Bob Dylan 10, Dickie Valentine 11, *Release Me*
12, Sandie Shaw 13, *Puppet on a String* 14, The Tremeloes 15, Brian Poole

QUIZ 278
POT LUCK

1 Which country was led by Lee Kuan Yew?

2 Out of which federation did he take his country?

3 What was Larissa Latynina's sport?

4 Who played a drunken crack-shot in *Cat Ballou*?

5 What kind of vehicle was a Moke?

6 Which novelist-to-be arrived in Britain from India in 1965?

7 By what name was James Wilson Vincent better known in the pop world?

8 Which actress tried to stab Sean Connery with her shoes?

9 What was the name of her villainous character?

10 Which film director made *The Birds*?

11 From whose story was it taken?

12 Who played Billy Liar on screen?

13 Which car maker's centenary was celebrated in 1963?

14 Who sang *Tie Me Kangaroo Down Sport*?

15 Who sang *Puff the Magic Dragon*?

ANSWERS

1, Singapore 2, Malaysia 3, Gymnastics 4, Lee Marvin 5, An all-terrain Mini car 6, Salman Rushdie 7, Jimmy Savile 8, Lotte Lenya (in *From Russia With Love*) 9, Rosa Klebb 10, Alfred Hitchcock 11, Daphne Du Maurier 12, Tom Courtenay 13, Henry Ford 14, Rolf Harris 15, Peter, Paul and Mary

QUIZ 279
SCIENCE & TECHNOLOGY

. . . .

1 The X-15 set a speed record in 1967. Was it a plane, a car, or a ship?

2 What crossed the Atlantic in 4 hours 46 minutes and 57 seconds in 1969?

3 What kind of surgical history did Christiaan Barnard make in 1967?

4 Otto Hahn (died 1960) was a) a pioneer of nuclear power, b) a German rocket scientist, c) the star of the first James Bond film?

5 Where did the first test flight of Concorde take place in March 1969: a) France b) Britain c) Australia?

6 Where was the British radio telescope that advanced space communications in the 60s?

7 Which British city had Europe's first moving pavement (in 1960)?

8 In what year was British Standard Time introduced as an experiment?

9 From which spacecraft did US astronaut Ed White walk in space in 1969?

10 What do the initials NASA stand for?

11 Which three pioneers of genetics won the 1962 Nobel Prize for medicine?

12 What year did John Glenn become the first American in orbit?

13 Which British scientist became only the third woman to win the Nobel Prize for Chemistry, in 1964?

14 What was a Thor-Delta: a) a rocket b) a railway locomotive or c) a nuclear power plant?

15 What was "Ariel 3"?

. . . .

ANSWERS

1, A plane 2, A Phantom jet fighter 3, First human heart transplant 4, a) A pioneer of nuclear power 5, a) France 6, Jodrell Bank 7, London, at the Bank underground station 8, 1967 9, "Gemini 4" 10, National Aeronautics and Space Administration 11, James Watson, Francis Crick and Maurice Wilkins 12, 1962 13, Dorothy Hodgkin 14, a) 15, Britain's first satellite, launched in 1967

QUIZ 280
WORLD EVENTS

• •

1 Whose murder in April 1968 shocked the world?

2 Who was stoned by an angry crowd in Harlem?

3 What was ELDO?

4 What were Britain's first decimal coins, launched in April 1968?

5 How much were they worth in old money?

6 Which drug was increasingly being seized in Western cities?

7 With which business were the Axel Springer group involved?

8 What happened to Ronan Point?

9 Which French university was closed because of riots?

10 Which country was brought to a standstill by spring disturbances and strikes?

11 Who declared he would not quit?

12 How did he fare in the subsequent election?

13 Which British art college was also in the news because of accusations of anarchy there?

14 Which surgical success took place at the National Heart Hospital in London?

15 Who was the recipient?

• •

ANSWERS

SPORT
1969

. . . .

1 Which Dutch team did AC Milan beat in the 1969 European Cup final?

2 Who won the 1969 Tour de France?

3 Who was the New York Jets star quarter back of 1969?

4 For whom did Don Rogers score a winning goal at Wembley?

5 Whom did they beat?

6 Which famous soccer club manager retired?

7 Who was named to succeed him?

8 What nationality was boxer José Napoles?

9 Which Scottish club completed the treble in 1969 (League, Cup, League Cup)?

10 Which cricket team dismissed the West Indies for only 25 runs?

11 Which Australian won his first British Open squash title in 1969?

12 For whom did Glenn Turner begin his Test career?

13 What sport did Roger Taylor play?

14 With whom did he have a reported changing room punch-up in Berlin?

15 Which batsman played his last Test for Pakistan in 1969?

. . . .

ANSWERS

POT LUCK

1 Who was known as Supermac?

2 Which politician spoke of "the white heat of technology"?

3 How many eyes had the night, according to singer Bobby Vee?

4 How long did it take John Ridgeway to row the Atlantic?

5 When?

6 And with whom?

7 At which university was Malcolm Rifkind in the 60s?

8 Which leading 60s actress was born in Doncaster in 1938?

9 What leather-clad role did she take on in 1965?

10 Which British artist won applause at the 1968 Vienna Biennale?

11 What cause did Geoffrey Rippon campaign for?

12 What honour was awarded to Flora Robson in 1960?

13 For what work?

14 Who recorded an album called *Beggar's Banquet*?

15 With what industry was Lord Rootes connected?

ANSWERS

1, Harold Macmillan 2, Harold Wilson 3, *A Thousand* 4, 92 days 5, 1966 6, Chay Blyth 7, Edinburgh 8, Diana Rigg 9, Emma Peel 10, Bridget Riley 11, British entry into Europe 12, Dame of the British Empire 13, Acting 14, The Rolling Stones 15, The car industry

QUIZ 283
ARTS & ENTERTAINMENT

1 Who led Herman's Hermits?

2 On which TV show was he spotted by a record producer?

3 Under what name did Sandra Goodrich become a pop star?

4 What was her trademark?

5 Which group did Andrew Loog Oldham manage?

6 Who were Cliff Bennett's group?

7 What was the Dave Clark Five's first hit?

8 Which country singer was king of the road in 1965?

9 Which record took the Stones to the top of the US charts in 1965?

10 What country were the Seekers from?

11 Who were Bill Medley and Bobby Hatfield?

12 Who chart-topped in the USA with *Where Did Our Love Go*?

13 Where was the Marquee Club: a) New York b) Liverpool c) London?

14 Who led The Famous Flames?

15 Who was singing *Fings Ain't Wot They Used To Be* in 1960?

ANSWERS

1. Peter Noone 2. *Coronation Street* 3. Sandie Shaw 4. She never wore shoes 5. The Rolling Stones 6. The Rebel Rousers 7. *Glad All Over* 8. Roger Miller 9. *Satisfaction* 10. Australia 11. The Righteous Brothers 12. The Supremes 13, c) London 14. James Brown 15. Max Bygraves

QUIZ 284
SCIENCE & TECHNOLOGY

∙ ∙

1 What went under the waves in 1965?

2 The Victor was a popular British car name; from which company?

3 Which British car maker made Anglias and Cortinas?

4 Which company introduced the Mustang to American drivers in 1964?

5 What year did Americans have to belt up?

6 Whose 1965 book *Unsafe at Any Speed* caused anxiety to motorists?

7 Which particular model was attacked in this book as unsafe?

8 When did the makers stop selling it?

9 What year did the US Congress pass its first law controlling exhaust pollution from cars?

10 What was the APT of 1969?

11 Where was it being planned?

12 What was unusual about its design?

13 What was significant about the maiden voyage of the "Savannah"?

14 What year was this maiden voyage?

15 Which spacecraft landed on the Moon in 1968?

∙ ∙

ANSWERS

1, "Sealab II" 2, Victor 3, Ford 4, Ford 5, 1968 6, Ralph Nader's 7, The Chevrolet Corvair 8, 1969 9, 1965 10, A planned high-speed train 11, Britain 12, It tilted when taking bends 13, It was the first nuclear-powered merchant ship 14, 1962 15, "Surveyor 7"

QUIZ 285
POT LUCK

• •

1 For which TV soap did Jack Rosenthal write scripts in the early 60s?

2 In which city was Leonard Rossiter born?

3 Which journalist earned the title "First Lady of Fleet Street"?

4 Bill Rogers became an MP in 1962: with which gang was he later associated?

5 Who died at her home at Sissinghurst Castle in 1961?

6 Which crime show began on British TV?

7 Who was the presenter most closely associated with this show?

8 What did Breton farmers dump in the road to protest about prices?

9 What did three prisoners use in 1962 to dig their way out of Alcatraz prison?

10 In which athletics event was Valeriy Brumel setting new heights?

11 What did 200 million people in Europe see for the first time in July 1962?

12 Which sports title did Karen Susman win (July 62)?

13 What did Fred Baldasare do underwater?

14 What was found beneath Downing Street in March 1962?

15 Which Princess was tempted by a return to the movies, but said no?

• •

ANSWERS

Monaco
1, *Coronation Street* 2, Liverpool 3, Jean Rook 4, The "Gang of Four", founders of the SDP in the 80s 5, Victoria Sackville West 6, *Police Five* 7, Shaw Taylor 8, Artichokes 9, Spoons 10, High jump 11, Live TV from the USA 12, Wimbledon women's singles 13, Swam the Channel 14, A human skull 15, Princess Grace of

QUIZ 286
SPORT
1969

• •

1 Which athletes complained their landings were too dangerous?

2 To which county did Ray Illingworth move at the age of 37?

3 Who was the 41-year-old wowing them at Wimbledon in 1969?

4 When had he last won a title there?

5 What was Ray Floyd's sport?

6 Who became manager of Ipswich Town soccer club?

7 Whose rugby tour was attacked by protesters?

8 What was the score in the 1969 Ryder Cup?

9 Who completed his second tennis Grand Slam in 1969?

10 Can you name the four players he beat … Australian title?

11 French?

12 Wimbledon?

13 United States?

14 In which spoort was John Spencer 1969 world champion?

15 Who were rugby's Five Nations champions in 1969?

• •

ANSWERS

QUIZ 287
POT LUCK

. . . .

1 Which future world champion won heavyweight boxing gold at the 1968 Olympics?

2 At which British car plant did women strike for equal pay in 1968?

3 Which refugees did President Johnson say in 1965 were welcome in the USA?

4 Which arms treaty was signed by 36 nations in 1968?

5 What did British MPs want made larger?

6 What was Union Gap Featuring Gary Puckett?

7 And what was their 1968 hit?

8 Which newspaper did Robert Maxwell want to buy in 1969?

9 Who sang *Lily the Pink*?

10 And what medicine did Lily invent, according to the lyrics?

11 Two London rail stations might have been merged, but weren't; which?

12 Why were the plans rejected?

13 Which animal featured in the 1969 film *Ring of Bright Water*?

14 What was the name of Disney's Beetle car?

15 Which TV travel show did Cliff Michelmore host?

. . . .

ANSWERS

1. George Foreman 2. Ford's Dagenham 3. Cubans 4. The nuclear non-proliferation treaty 5. The Parliament buildings 6. An American pop group 7. *Young Girl* 8. *The News of the World* 9. Scaffold 10. Medicinal compound 11. King's Cross and St Pancras 12. Too costly 13. Otter 14. Herbie 15. Holiday

POT LUCK

. . . .

1   Which member of the Monty Python team usually wrote alone?

2   Whose ice hockey team beat Russia 4-3 in 1969?

3   What happened to the Governor-general of Guyana in 1969?

4   What were four Southern states told to end by the US Federal government?

5   Which illness killed hundreds of people in Britain during the winter of 1969?

6   Who "heard it through the grapevine" in 1969?

7   Which part of Britain did Amen Corner come from?

8   Who was the group's lead singer?

9   Whose brother was Mike McGear?

10 Who shared the credit on the Beatles' hit *Get Back*?

11 Was he a) American b) British or c) Australian?

12 Which boot style remained fashionable through the 60s for women?

13 What was Britain's first reggae number one?

14 By?

15 Which 60s carmaker made the Viva and Viscount?

. . . .

ANSWERS

1. Eric Idle 2. Czechoslovakia 3. Scaffolding fell and killed him 4. Segregation 5. Flu 6. Marvin Gaye 7. Wales 8. Andy Fairweather-Low 9. Paul McCartney's 10. Billy Preston 11. a) American 12. Long boots 13. *The Israelites* 14. Desmond Dekker and the Aces 15. Vauxhall

WORLD EVENTS

1 Why were more people than usual in Mexico City in 1968?

2 Who met on board "HMS Fearless"?

3 What did President Johnson order stopped in November 1968?

4 Which US politician had called for the war to be scaled down?

5 Which Warsaw Pact leaders were summoned to Moscow for a telling off?

6 Which country banned an England cricketer and so lost a tour visit?

7 Who was the controversial cricketer?

8 Where was Richard Daley mayor?

9 What drug addiction was said by a leading expert to be a major emergency?

10 Who got to the White House at last in November?

11 Whom had he defeated?

12 Who were the two vice-presidential runners?

13 Who set off to fly around the Moon?

14 Whose crew came home from captivity?

15 Which 11-year-old received a life sentence for manslaughter in Britain?

ANSWERS

1, The Olympic Games opened 2, Harold Wilson and Ian Smith 3, Bombing of North Vietnam 4, Richard Nixon 5, The Czechs 6, South Africa 7, Basil D'Oliveira, who was South African by birth 8, Chicago 9, Heroin 10, Richard Nixon 11, Hubert Humphrey 12, Spiro Agnew (Nixon) and Edmund Muskie (Humphrey) 13, The crew of "Apollo 8" 14, The crew of the spy ship "Pueblo" 15, Mary Bell

WORLD EVENTS

1 Why were more people than usual in Mexico City in 1968?

2 Who met on board HMS *Fearless*?

3 What did President Johnson order stopped in November 1968?

4 Which US politician had called for the war to be scaled down?

5 Which Warsaw Pact leaders were summoned to Moscow for a telling off?

6 Which country banned an England cricketer and so lost a tour visit?

7 Who was the controversial cricketer?

8 Where was Richard Daley mayor?

9 What drug addiction was said by a leading expert to be a major emergency?

10 Who got to the White House at last in November 1968?

11 Whom had he defeated?

12 Who were the two vice-presidential runners?

13 Who set off to fly around the Moon?

14 Whose crew came home from captivity?

15 Which 11-year-old received a life sentence for manslaughter in Britain?

ANSWERS

1, The Olympic Games opened 2, Harold Wilson and Ian Smith 3, Bombing of North Vietnam 4, Richard Nixon 5, The Czechs 6, South Africa 7, Basil D'Oliveira, who was South African by birth 8, Chicago 9, Heroin 10, Richard Nixon 11, Hubert Humphrey 12, Spiro Agnew (Nixon) and Edmund Muskie (Humphrey) 13, The crew of Apollo 8 14, The crew of the spy ship "Pueblo" 15, Mary Bell

QUIZ 291
SCIENCE & TECHNOLOGY

• •

1 What was the name of the US Navy's first nuclear-powered aircraft carrier?

2 What were there 225 million of in 1969?

3 Which ship entered New York on her maiden voyage in May 1969?

4 What kind of craft was the SR-N4?

5 What did astronomers Hewish and Bell discover in 1968?

6 In America in 1969, how many cars out of 100 were foreign imports: a) 27 b) 38 or c) 11?

7 Which car maker introduced the Maverick and Capri models in 1969?

8 What destroyed *Apollo 1* in 1967?

9 How many astronauts were killed?

10 Who were they?

11 Where was Australia's Casey Station, opened in 1969?

12 Who or what was Bonny, launched into space in 1969?

13 What kind of craft was *ESSA*?

14 What did the initials OAO stand for in space terms?

15 Where in Australia was the rocket testing ground used by British space scientists?

• •

ANSWERS

1. Enterprise 2. Telephones 3. The *QE2* 4. A hovercraft 5. Pulsars 6. c) 11 7. Ford 8. Fire at Cape Kennedy 9. Three 10. Virgil Grissom, Roger Chaffee, Edward White 11. Antarctica 12. A monkey 13. A weather satellite 14. Orbiting Astronomical Observatory 15. Woomera

NOTES

NOTES

....

NOTES

NOTES

· ·

NOTES

. . . .

NOTES

....

NOTES

. . . .

NOTES

NOTES

....

NOTES

....

NOTES

NOTES

....

NOTES

....